UNLOCKING YOUR ALL

UNLOCKING YOUR ALL

Dr. *A*. Romani

Authored Pages
Mt. Prospect, Il USA | 1 (888) 821-3271 | AuthoredPages.com

Copyright © 2025 **Dr. A. Romani**. All Rights Reserved.

Published by **Dr. A. Romani** / Authored Pages

ISBN 979-8-9990430-4-7

Unlocking Your All

No part of this work covered by the copy herein may be distributed or reproduced in any type of form or by any means, except as permitted by the U.S. Copyright law(s), without the prior written permission of the copyright owner or publisher.

ISBN: 979-8-9990430-4-7 (print, paperback PB)
ISBN: 979-8-9990430-5-4 (ebook)

Library of Congress Control Number 2025914875

BISAC: SEL004000 | SEL021000 | SEL031000

The information presented does not constitute health or medical advice. The content of this book is for informational purposes only and is not intended to diagnose, treat, cure, or prevent any condition or disease.

Dedication

This book is dedicated to those who have faced adversity, risen, and learned from their mistakes. It is for those who believe in transformation and seek to unlock their full potential. It is also for those who have felt self-doubt and struggled to find their place in the world. The book offers hope and a pathway to self-discovery for those who choose self-compassion over self-judgment. It is also for dreamers, visionaries, and innovators who refuse to settle for mediocrity and embrace the journey of self-discovery as a lifelong pursuit. The book is dedicated to the reader, who embarks on this journey of self-improvement, expressing courage, self-belief, and commitment to creating a life of purpose and fulfillment.

Table of Contents

1. Introduction
2. Description
3. Chapter 1: Understanding Your Inner Landscape (pg. *1*)
    1) Identifying Limiting Beliefs (p. *6*)
    2) Uncovering Your Strengths and Resources (p. *21*)
    3) Building Self-Compassion (p.*36*)
    4) Cultivating A Growth Mindset (pg. *50*)
    5) Setting Realistic Goals and Expectations (pg. *65*)
4. Chapter 2: Enhancing Your Productivity (p. *79*)
    1) Time Management Technics (p. *79*)
    2) Effective Organization Strategies (p. 94)
    3) Minimize Distractions and Procrastination (p.108)
    4) Building Effective Habits (p. *123*)
    5) Leveraging Technology for Productivity (p. *136*)

5. Chapter 3: Mastering Your Social Interactions (p.*150*)
    1) Improving Communication Skills (p.*150*)
    2) Building and Maintaining Healthy Relationships (p.*171*)
    3) Overcoming Social Anxiety (p.*188*)
    4) Networking and Building Connections (p.*201*)
    5) Setting Boundaries in Relationships (p.*218*)
6. Chapter 4: Achieving Your Goals and Aspirations (p. *234*)
    1) Goal Setting and Action Planning (p.*234*)
    2) Overcoming Obstacles and Setbacks (p. *249*)
    3) Maintaining Motivation and Momentum (p.*260*)
    4) Celebrating Success and Recognizing Progress (p.*272*)
    5) Building a Support System (p.*284*)
7. Chapter 5: Cultivation Lasting Personal Growth (p. *301*)
    1) Developing Self-Awareness (p. *301*)
    2) Embracing Continuous Learning (p.*317*)
    3) Practicing Self-Care and Well-being (p.*330*)
    4) Maintaining a Positive Mindset (p. *347*)
    5) Giving Back and Contributing to Others (p. *362*)
8. Acknowledgments (p. 376)
9. Glossary (p. *377*)
10. Biography (p.*378*)

Introduction

Unleash the extraordinary potential within you! In "*Unlocking Your All*," embark on a transformative journey that will guide you through the intricate pathways of your mind and spirit. Discover powerful techniques to harness your innate abilities, ignite your passions, and break free from the limitations holding you back. With practical insights and inspiration on every page, this book is your key to awakening the unstoppable force that lies in each of us. Are you ready to unlock your true power?... Then your journey starts now!

Description

Uncover the extraordinary potential within you in "*Unlocking Your All*," a transformative guide that empowers readers to navigate the intricate pathways of their mind and spirit, unlocking innate abilities and passions along the way. Set against the backdrop of personal growth and self-discovery, this insightful book invites you into a world where every limitation becomes an opportunity. As you delve into the chapters, you will encounter practical techniques designed to ignite your passions and shatter the barriers that hold you back. From mindfulness exercises to empowering affirmations, each page offers you tools to awaken the unstoppable force that lies dormant within. The book guides you through critical moments of reflection and action, emphasizing how small, consistent changes can lead to monumental shifts in your life. What sets "*Unlocking Your All*" apart is its blend of motivational insights and actionable advice, making it perfect for anyone seeking a roadmap to personal fulfillment. This book stands as a unique companion in the vast landscape of self-help literature. Are you ready to transform your life and unleash your true potential? Then your journey can start now—grab your copy of "*Unlocking Your All*" and step into the life you've always dreamed of!

Chapter 1: Understanding Your Inner Landscape

This book is dedicated to the quiet revolutionaries, the unsung heroes of self-improvement, the individuals who dare to dream bigger, strive harder, and persevere longer. It's for those who have faced adversity head-on, who have stumbled and risen, who have learned from their mistakes and emerged stronger. This is for the courageous souls who believe in the power of transformation, who refuse to let their challenges define them, and who actively seek to unlock their full potential.

It is dedicated to those who have felt the sting of self-doubt, the weight of insecurity, and the overwhelming feeling of being lost in the labyrinth of life's complexities. To those who have questioned their worth, doubted their abilities, and struggled to find their place in the world, this book offers a beacon of hope, a pathway to self-discovery, and a roadmap to a more fulfilling existence.

This dedication extends to the silent warriors battling inner demons, fighting their way through the shadows of self-criticism and negative self-talk. You, the resilient souls who consistently choose self-compassion over self-judgment, deserve profound admiration for your unwavering dedication to personal growth. Your journey is a testament to the strength of the human spirit, a beacon illuminating the path for others to follow.

It's for the dreamers, the visionaries, the innovators – those who refuse to settle for mediocrity, who are driven by a burning desire to make a difference, to leave their mark on the world. To those who embrace the journey of self-discovery as a lifelong pursuit, understanding that the destination is not the only reward; it is the continuous process of learning, growing, and evolving.

Finally, this book is dedicated to you – the reader. Your willingness to embark on this journey of self-improvement is a testament to your courage, your self-belief, and your commitment to creating a life of purpose, meaning, and lasting fulfillment. May these pages serve as a catalyst for profound personal transformation, empowering you to unleash your inner strength, embrace your authentic self, and live a life that is truly extraordinary. May this book be a testament to your unwavering commitment to growth and transformation. May it be a source of inspiration, guidance, and encouragement as you navigate the path towards self-mastery and the realization of your dreams. You deserve this journey, and I am so very honored to be part of it.

Identifying Limiting Beliefs

Our journey towards unlocking our full potential begins with a deep understanding of our inner landscape. This isn't about unearthing hidden secrets or dwelling on past traumas; rather, it's about cultivating a clear, honest view of our beliefs, strengths, and weaknesses. I want you to know this self-awareness is the foundation upon which we build a life of purpose, fulfillment, and lasting happiness. One crucial aspect of this inner exploration is identifying and challenging our limiting beliefs.

Limiting beliefs are those ingrained thought patterns and assumptions that hold us back from achieving our goals and living the life we desire. They are often deeply rooted, subconscious, and operate subtly, influencing our decisions and actions without our conscious awareness. These beliefs are not necessarily factual; they are interpretations of experiences shaped by our past, our upbringing, and societal conditioning. They act as invisible barriers, hindering our progress and preventing us from reaching our full potential.

Think of your mind as fertile ground. What seeds have been planted there? Are they seeds of self-doubt, fear, or inadequacy? Or are they seeds of confidence, resilience, and self-belief? Limiting beliefs often manifest as negative self-talk, a persistent feeling of inadequacy, or a sense of helplessness in the face of challenges. These beliefs can manifest in various ways, including:

"I'm not good enough": This pervasive belief undermines self-worth and prevents individuals from pursuing opportunities or taking risks. It stems from a deep-seated insecurity often rooted in childhood experiences, comparisons with others, or critical feedback received throughout life. It's a belief that needs to be challenged by focusing on accomplishments, no matter how small, and actively reframing negative self-talk.

"I'm not smart enough": This belief can hinder learning and personal growth. It can lead to avoidance of challenges and a reluctance to step outside one's comfort zone. It's important to remember that intelligence is not fixed; it's a dynamic capacity that can be developed and enhanced through learning and perseverance. Celebrate your progress and acknowledge the growth you've achieved.

"I'm not worthy of success": This limiting belief often manifests as self-sabotage, a subconscious tendency to undermine one's own efforts to prevent success. It's usually rooted in deeply ingrained feelings of unworthiness or insecurity. The key to overcoming this is to build self-compassion, acknowledge your strengths, and redefine your perception of worthiness, understanding it's not tied to external achievements but to your inherent value as a human being.

"I'm not capable of change": This belief fosters a sense of helplessness and resignation. It prevents individuals from taking proactive steps towards self-improvement. Challenging this belief requires fostering a growth mindset, acknowledging your capacity for adaptation, and celebrating every step of progress.

"It's too late for me": This belief often emerges in later life, preventing people from pursuing dreams they believed were unattainable or beyond their reach. The reality is that it's never too late to pursue a passion, learn a new skill, or reinvent yourself. Focus on the present and what you can achieve today.

Identifying these limiting beliefs requires honest self-reflection. Journaling can be a powerful tool. Take some time each day to write down your thoughts and feelings. Pay attention to recurring negative patterns and themes. Are there certain situations that consistently trigger self-doubt or feelings of inadequacy? What are the underlying beliefs that fuel these feelings?

Now, another effective method is to monitor your self-talk. Become aware of the inner voice that constantly criticizes or judges you. What messages is it sending? And, are these messages helpful or maybe harmful? Write them down. Once you've identified these negative messages, you can begin to challenge and reframe them.

Consider seeking feedback from trusted friends, family members, or a therapist. Sometimes, an outside perspective can illuminate patterns and beliefs we are blind to. They might be able to point out instances where our limiting beliefs are holding us back, offering valuable insights and support.

Challenging these beliefs is not a one-time event; it's an ongoing process. Start by questioning the validity of each negative thought. Is there evidence to support it? Often, there isn't. These beliefs are often based on assumptions, fears, and past experiences that may no longer be relevant.

Replace negative thoughts with positive affirmations. Affirmations are positive statements that can help reprogram your subconscious mind. Repeat them regularly, and believe in their truth. Visualize yourself achieving your goals. What does it feel like? How does it look? Visualizations can help strengthen your belief in your ability to overcome obstacles and achieve success.

For example, if you believe "I'm not good enough," you can replace it with "I am capable and worthy of success." If you believe "I'm not smart enough," you can replace it with "I am intelligent and capable of learning anything I set my mind to." These affirmations, repeated consistently, will begin to rewire your thinking patterns and foster a more positive self-image.

It's also crucial to celebrate your successes, no matter how small. Acknowledge your accomplishments and recognize your progress. This helps build self-confidence and reinforce your belief in your ability to achieve your goals. Focus on your strengths, and build on them. What are you naturally good at? What do you enjoy doing? Cultivating your strengths will not only boost your self-esteem but also equip you with the resources to overcome challenges.

Remember, the journey to understanding and overcoming your limiting beliefs is a marathon, not a sprint. Be patient with yourself, celebrate your progress, and don't be discouraged by setbacks. Each step you take, each limiting belief you challenge, brings you closer to living a life of purpose, fulfillment, and lasting happiness. Embrace the power of self-awareness, and embark on this transformative journey towards a more empowered and authentic you. The path may be challenging, but the rewards are immeasurable. The freedom you'll experience by releasing these limitations will be transformative and deeply rewarding. It's about reclaiming your narrative and maybe writing a story of success, happiness, and fulfillment. Believe in your ability to change, and you will.

This process of identifying and challenging limiting beliefs is integral to building self-awareness. It's about acknowledging the power of our thoughts and how they shape our experiences. By recognizing and reframing these negative beliefs, we pave the way for personal growth, increased productivity, and the achievement of our aspirations. This process will be an ongoing one, requiring patience, self-compassion, and a commitment to personal growth. But remember, the journey itself is part of the reward. The more you understand yourself, the better equipped you will be to navigate life's challenges and achieve your full potential. Remember to treat yourself with kindness and understanding throughout this process. It's okay to make mistakes; it's part of learning and growing. Celebrate your progress, no matter how small, and never give up on yourself. You have the power within you to overcome any obstacle and create the life you desire. Believe in yourself, and the rest will follow. You have to remember, the strength you seek resides within you, waiting to be unleashed.

Uncovering Your Strengths and Your Resources

Now that we've begun to explore the landscape of our limiting beliefs, let's shift our focus to the more empowering aspects of our inner world: our strengths and resources. Just as identifying and challenging our negative thought patterns is crucial, recognizing and leveraging our positive attributes is equally important for personal growth and achieving our goals. This isn't about boasting or becoming self-absorbed; rather, it's about acknowledging our inherent capabilities and utilizing them effectively to navigate life's challenges and reach our full potential.

Many of us undervalue our strengths, often focusing more on our perceived weaknesses. We may downplay our accomplishments, minimizing our successes and dwelling on our failures. This tendency stems from various factors, including societal expectations, perfectionism, and a lack of self-compassion. However, understanding our strengths is essential to building self-confidence, enhancing productivity, and achieving our aspirations.

So, how do we uncover these often-hidden strengths? The process involves introspection, self-reflection, and a willingness to honestly assess our capabilities. One effective method is to engage in mindful self-observation. Pay attention to your daily activities, noticing what tasks you enjoy, what you excel at, and what comes naturally to you. What do people consistently compliment you on? What areas of your life bring you a sense of accomplishment and satisfaction? These are all potential indicators of your strengths.

Another powerful tool is to seek feedback from others. Ask trusted friends, family members, colleagues, or mentors to share their observations of your strengths. Their perspectives can offer valuable insights that you might have overlooked. Consider asking some specific questions, such as: "What are some of my key skills or talents?" or "What am I good at?" and maybe "What do you admire about me?" Be open to their responses, even if they highlight areas you hadn't previously considered.

Additionally, consider taking personality assessments or aptitude tests. While these tools shouldn't be the sole basis for determining your strengths, they can provide valuable insights into your personality traits, preferences, and abilities. Many free and paid assessments are available online, ranging from widely known personality tests like Myers-Briggs to more specialized assessments focusing on specific skills or career paths. Remember to approach these assessments with a critical yet open mind, using them as a starting point for further exploration rather than definitive judgments.

Once you've identified your strengths, it's crucial to understand how they can be leveraged for personal and professional growth. Consider how these strengths translate to different areas of your life. For example, if you possess strong communication skills, how can you utilize them to enhance your relationships, your career, or your community involvement? If you are a creative problem-solver, how can you apply this skill to tackle challenges in your personal or professional life? The key is to actively seek opportunities to use your strengths, transforming them into tangible assets that drive progress and fulfillment.

Furthermore, consider how you can develop and strengthen your existing strengths. Just as we challenge and overcome our limiting beliefs, we can also nurture and expand our inherent capabilities. This might involve seeking additional training, engaging in continuous learning, or taking on new challenges that stretch your abilities. The process of growth is ongoing, and by continuously honing your skills and talents, you build even greater self-confidence and enhance your ability to overcome obstacles.

Beyond your inherent strengths, consider the resources available to you. These resources can be internal or external, tangible or intangible. Internal resources might include your resilience, your determination, your self-discipline, and your problem-solving abilities. These are the inner strengths you've cultivated over time and which fuel your journey towards self-improvement. They represent your internal capacity for growth and adaptation. Cultivating these internal resources is a vital aspect of personal development, forming the bedrock of your ability to meet challenges with confidence and determination.

External resources are equally important. These could include your support network – friends, family, mentors, colleagues, or therapists who offer guidance, encouragement, and practical assistance. They represent the invaluable human connections that contribute to our emotional well-being and provide a crucial support system for navigating life's challenges. Don't underestimate the power of seeking support when facing difficulties. And know that this isn't a sign of weakness; it's a sign of strength and self-awareness.

Consider also tangible resources such as your financial resources, your time, your access to information and technology, or your physical health. These resources provide the practical tools and support needed to achieve your goals. A careful assessment of your available resources, coupled with strategic planning, will facilitate the efficient use of your resources to maximize their impact in pursuing your goals.

For instance, if your goal is to start a small business, your external resources might include your savings, access to business loans, or mentorship from experienced entrepreneurs. Internal resources such as your resilience, problem-solving skills, and self-discipline are equally vital in navigating the challenges of entrepreneurship. A realistic appraisal of both internal and external resources is crucial for successful planning and execution.

Once you have identified both your strengths and resources, it's time to create a plan to leverage them effectively. This involves setting clear goals and identifying the steps needed to achieve them, considering how your strengths and available resources can facilitate your progress. For example, if your goal is to improve your physical fitness, you might use your self-discipline as an internal resource and access to a gym or fitness classes as an external resource. Your inherent athletic ability, if any, would also be a significant internal strength to utilize. Effective planning involves understanding your limitations as well as your strengths, ensuring your goals are realistic and achievable given your available resources.

Remember, your strengths and resources are not static; they can evolve and expand over time. As you grow and learn, new strengths will emerge, and your access to resources might increase. The key is to remain open to new possibilities, to embrace continuous learning, and to continually assess your strengths and resources to adjust your approach as needed. This dynamic approach to self-assessment ensures that you remain adaptable and resourceful as you navigate your personal and professional journey.

The process of uncovering your strengths and resources is an ongoing journey of self-discovery. It requires honest self-reflection, a willingness to seek feedback, and a commitment to continuous growth. By understanding and leveraging your unique capabilities and available resources, you build a strong foundation for achieving your goals and living a fulfilling life. Embrace this journey of self-discovery, and you will be amazed at the power and potential that resides within you, waiting to be unleashed. Remember, this journey is about celebrating your inherent worth and capabilities. It's about embracing your uniqueness and understanding that you possess the tools necessary to create the life you desire. The power to shape your future is within your grasp. Believe in yourself, trust in your abilities, and use your strengths and resources to create a life of purpose, fulfillment, and lasting happiness.

Building Self-Compassion

Building self-compassion is not about self-indulgence or ignoring our flaws; instead, it's about cultivating a relationship with ourselves that is characterized by kindness, understanding, and acceptance. It's about treating ourselves with the same empathy and compassion we would offer a dear friend struggling with similar challenges. This shift in perspective is transformative, which is allowing us to navigate difficulties with greater resilience and even self-assurance.

Many of us are far too critical of ourselves, constantly berating ourselves for perceived failures or shortcomings. This inner critic, often fueled by perfectionistic tendencies and negative self-talk, can be incredibly damaging to our self-esteem and overall well-being. It creates a vicious cycle of self-doubt and negativity, hindering our ability to learn from mistakes and move forward. To break free from this cycle, we must learn to approach our imperfections with kindness and understanding.

One powerful technique for cultivating self-compassion is mindful self-reflection. This involves taking time each day to pause, breathe, and observe our inner world without judgment. Notice the thoughts, feelings, and sensations arising within you, acknowledging them without trying to change or suppress them. This practice helps us become more aware of our inner critic and its patterns, allowing us to gently challenge its harsh judgments.

For example, if you make a mistake at work, instead of immediately launching into self-criticism ("I'm such an idiot! I'll never get promoted!"), pause and take a few deep breaths. Acknowledge the mistake without judgment ("I made a mistake. It's not ideal, but it's happened"). Then, consider what you can learn from the experience and how you can prevent similar mistakes in the future. Treat yourself with the same understanding and compassion you'd offer a friend who had made a similar error.

Another crucial aspect of self-compassion involves recognizing our shared humanity. We all make mistakes, experience setbacks, and struggle with challenges. It's a universal human experience. Remembering this helps us to avoid isolating ourselves in our struggles and to see our imperfections as part of the larger human experience. This perspective shift allows us to approach our challenges with greater empathy and self-acceptance.

Consider times when you have offered compassion to a friend or loved one facing a difficult situation. Recall the kindness, understanding, and empathy you extended to them. Now, apply those same qualities to yourself. Treat yourself with the same level of understanding and support you would offer someone you care about.

Practicing self-compassion requires conscious effort and consistent practice. It's not a quick fix, but a gradual process of learning to treat ourselves with greater kindness and acceptance. One helpful technique is to engage in self-compassionate self-talk. Instead of using harsh, critical language ("I'm a failure"), replace it with kind, supportive language ("I'm having a tough time right now, but I'm learning and growing").

For instance, if you're struggling to meet a deadline, instead of berating yourself for your lack of productivity, try saying something like, "This is challenging, but I'm doing my best, and that's enough for now." Such affirmations, while seemingly simple, can significantly impact our emotional state, reducing self-criticism and fostering self-acceptance.

Self-compassion also involves being mindful of our physical needs. When we're struggling emotionally, our physical well-being often suffers. We may neglect our sleep, our diet, or our exercise routine. Prioritizing self-care – getting enough sleep, eating nourishing food, and engaging in regular physical activity – is vital for emotional well-being and resilience. This act of caring for our physical needs demonstrates self-compassion in action.

Consider incorporating regular mindfulness practices into your routine. Mindfulness meditation, yoga, or even simply spending time in nature can help us connect with our inner selves and cultivate a sense of calm and self-acceptance. These practices help us to observe our thoughts and feelings without judgment, promoting self-awareness and empathy for our inner experiences.

Furthermore, engage in activities that bring you joy and a sense of accomplishment. This could be anything from spending time with loved ones to pursuing a hobby to volunteering in your community. These activities help us reconnect with our strengths and foster a sense of purpose, which are crucial for building self-esteem and self-compassion.

Remember, setbacks and challenges are inevitable parts of life. How we respond to them shapes our experience and determines our level of resilience. By cultivating self-compassion, we approach these difficulties with greater kindness, understanding, and acceptance, empowering ourselves to learn from our mistakes, bounce back from setbacks, and move forward with renewed strength and determination.

Self-compassion is not a passive act; it's an active practice requiring consistent effort and dedication. It's a journey of self-discovery and self-acceptance, a process of learning to treat ourselves with the same kindness, empathy, and understanding we readily offer to others. As we cultivate self-compassion, we develop greater emotional resilience, fostering a stronger sense of self-worth and enhancing our ability to navigate life's inevitable challenges. This journey of self-compassion is an investment in our overall well-being, leading to a more fulfilling and meaningful life.

It's important to note that building self-compassion is not a linear process. There will be times when you slip back into self-criticism, and that's perfectly normal. The key is to acknowledge these moments without judgment, to gently redirect your thoughts towards self-compassion, and to continue practicing self-kindness and acceptance.

Consider keeping a journal to track your progress in cultivating self-compassion. Write down your thoughts and feelings, noting instances where you've been kind to yourself and instances where you've been self-critical. This practice can help you to become more aware of your patterns of self-talk and to identify areas where you can improve. You can also use your journal to reflect on your successes and challenges, helping you maintain perspective and motivation as you continue your journey.

Finally, remember that seeking support is a sign of strength, not weakness. If you're struggling to cultivate self-compassion on your own, don't hesitate to reach out to a therapist or counselor. A mental health professional can provide guidance and support as you navigate this process, helping you develop healthy coping mechanisms and strategies for managing self-criticism. They can offer tailored strategies and exercises to help you specifically address your challenges and build a foundation of self-compassion. Remember, building a life of greater self-compassion is a worthwhile investment in your happiness and well-being. Embrace the journey, and celebrate your progress along the way. The path to self-compassion is a journey of self-discovery, offering the potential for profound personal growth and a richer, more fulfilling life.

Cultivating a Growth Mindset

Building upon the foundation of self-compassion, we now turn our attention to cultivating a growth mindset. This isn't simply about positive thinking; it's about fundamentally altering how we perceive challenges, setbacks, and our own capabilities.

A growth mindset, rooted in the belief that our abilities are malleable and can be developed through dedication and hard work, is the cornerstone of personal and professional success. It's the key to unlocking our potential and achieving our goals, no matter how ambitious they may seem.

Unlike a fixed mindset, which views abilities as innate and unchangeable, a growth mindset embraces the power of learning and improvement. Individuals with a fixed mindset often avoid challenges, fearing failure will confirm their perceived limitations. They tend to interpret criticism negatively, viewing it as a reflection of their inherent inadequacy, and give up easily in the face of obstacles. They often focus on proving their intelligence rather than expanding it.

In contrast, those with a growth mindset see challenges as opportunities for growth and learning. They view setbacks not as failures, but as valuable feedback, providing insights into areas needing improvement. They embrace criticism as constructive feedback, using it to refine their skills and knowledge. They persist despite obstacles, understanding that effort and perseverance are key to mastery.

Their focus is on learning and growing, not simply proving their intelligence.

The transition from a fixed to a growth mindset is a conscious and continuous process. It requires consistent effort and a willingness to challenge our deeply ingrained beliefs about ourselves and our capabilities. This shift in perspective involves actively seeking out challenges, viewing mistakes as learning opportunities, and embracing feedback as a means of improvement.

One powerful strategy for fostering a growth mindset is to actively challenge our negative self-talk. When faced with a challenge, we often engage in self-doubt and pessimism.

We might say things like, "I'm not good enough," or "I'll never be able to do this." These thoughts reinforce a fixed mindset, hindering our ability to persist and achieve our goals. To counteract this negative self-talk, we need to consciously replace these self-limiting beliefs with more positive and empowering affirmations.

Instead of saying "I'm not good enough," try saying "I'm still learning, and I'll keep improving." Instead of saying "I'll never be able to do this," try saying "This will be challenging, but I'm willing to put in the effort to learn and succeed." These subtle shifts in language can have a profound impact on our motivation, resilience, and overall performance. Affirmations act as mental reframing; by repeating them consistently, we can gradually reshape our beliefs and foster a growth mindset.

Another crucial element of cultivating a growth mindset is focusing on the process rather than solely on the outcome. When we're solely focused on achieving a specific outcome, setbacks can be devastating. We might feel discouraged and give up easily.

However, if we focus on the process of learning and improving, setbacks become less significant. We can view them as opportunities to learn from our mistakes and refine our approach.

For example, if you're learning a new language, focus on the daily practice, on mastering new vocabulary and grammar rules, and on enjoying the process of learning. Don't solely fixate on the ultimate goal of fluency. Celebrate small victories, such as successfully understanding a complex sentence or holding a conversation with a native speaker. This process-oriented approach helps maintain motivation and resilience, fostering a growth mindset even when progress is slow or uneven.

Embracing feedback is also critical for developing a growth mindset. Feedback, whether positive or negative, provides valuable insights into our strengths and weaknesses. It allows us to identify areas for improvement and refine our skills and knowledge. Individuals with a fixed mindset often perceive feedback as a personal attack, rejecting criticism and becoming defensive.

In contrast, those with a growth mindset view feedback as an opportunity to learn and grow. They actively seek out feedback from others, using it to enhance their performance.

This active pursuit of feedback might involve seeking constructive criticism from mentors, colleagues, or friends. It could involve self-assessment, honestly evaluating our strengths and weaknesses, identifying areas where we can improve, and creating a plan to address these areas. Regular self-reflection, perhaps through journaling, allows us to identify patterns in our behavior and thoughts, revealing areas where we can apply a growth mindset to greater effect.

Furthermore, it's vital to surround ourselves with people who encourage and support our growth. Our social environment plays a significant role in shaping our mindset. If we're surrounded by people who constantly criticize or discourage us, it's difficult to maintain a positive and growth-oriented perspective. However, if we're surrounded by individuals who offer support, encouragement, and constructive feedback, it becomes easier to embrace challenges and persevere through setbacks.

Consider actively seeking out mentors or role models who embody a growth mindset. Observe their behaviors, their approaches to challenges, and how they respond to setbacks. Their resilience and dedication can be incredibly inspiring, reinforcing your own commitment to cultivating a growth mindset.

Cultivating a growth mindset is also about embracing the power of learning. It's about viewing learning as an ongoing process, not a destination. It's about constantly seeking new knowledge and skills, challenging ourselves to step outside of our comfort zones, and embracing the challenges that come with personal and professional growth. This might involve taking courses, reading books, attending workshops, or engaging in other forms of lifelong learning. The commitment to continuous learning is a powerful testament to the growth mindset.

It's important to remember that cultivating a growth mindset isn't a one-time event but a continuous process. There will be times when we revert to a fixed mindset, when self-doubt creeps in, and when we question our abilities. This is perfectly normal. The key is to recognize these moments, acknowledge our self-limiting beliefs, and consciously redirect our thoughts towards a growth-oriented perspective. Use those moments as opportunities for self-reflection and to reinforce your commitment to the growth mindset.

One practical technique to maintain this focus is through regular goal setting.

Set both short-term and long-term goals that challenge you but are also achievable. Break down large goals into smaller, more manageable steps, and regularly track your progress. Celebrating small victories along the way will help you stay motivated and reinforce your belief in your ability to grow and learn.

Another technique involves visualizing success. Imagine yourself achieving your goals, experiencing the positive feelings associated with success, and feeling confident in your abilities. This visualization can help build your confidence and resilience, enabling you to approach challenges with greater optimism and determination.

Finally, remember that embracing a growth mindset is a journey, not a destination. There will be ups and downs, setbacks and breakthroughs. The important thing is to keep learning, keep growing, and keep moving forward. The rewards of cultivating a growth mindset—increased resilience, enhanced self-esteem, and the ability to achieve your goals—are well worth the effort. Embrace the process, celebrate your progress, and remember that your potential is limitless.

Setting Realistic pals and Expectations

Building upon the foundation of self-compassion and a growth mindset, we now arrive at a crucial step in understanding your inner landscape: setting realistic goals and expectations. This isn't about diminishing your ambition, but rather about crafting a roadmap to success that's both challenging and achievable. Unrealistic goals often lead to discouragement, frustration, and ultimately, abandonment of your aspirations. Realistic goals, on the other hand, provide a framework for consistent progress, fostering a sense of accomplishment and fueling your motivation to continue.

The key to setting realistic goals lies in understanding your current capabilities and resources. Honest self-assessment is paramount. Consider your strengths, weaknesses, available time, resources, and potential obstacles. This isn't about self-criticism; it's about gaining a clear perspective on your starting point. For example, if you're aiming to write a novel, assess your current writing skills, available writing time, and any potential distractions or commitments that might interfere with your progress. Don't just dream of finishing the novel; develop a realistic plan considering your current capabilities.

Breaking down large goals into smaller, manageable steps is a powerful technique for setting realistic expectations. Instead of aiming for the summit of a mountain in one leap, focus on reaching the first base camp, then the next, and so on. Each small achievement serves as a building block, providing motivation and a tangible sense of progress. This approach is particularly effective for long-term goals that might seem daunting at first glance.

For instance, if your goal is to run a marathon, instead of immediately aiming for a full *26.2* miles, start with shorter runs, gradually increasing the distance and intensity over time. Celebrate each milestone—finishing your first *5k*, then your first *10k*, and so on. This incremental approach keeps you motivated and prevents burnout, allowing you to steadily work towards your ultimate goal. The sense of accomplishment from each smaller achievement fuels your determination to continue.

This process of breaking down larger goals into smaller steps also allows for flexibility and adaptation. Life is unpredictable, and unforeseen circumstances can sometimes derail our plans. By breaking your goals into smaller components, you can more easily adjust your approach if necessary. For example, if an unexpected illness prevents you from running for a week, it won't derail your entire marathon training plan. You can simply adjust your schedule and pick up where you left off.

Realistic goal-setting also requires considering the potential obstacles you might encounter. Identify potential roadblocks and develop contingency plans to overcome them. This proactive approach minimizes the chances of setbacks derailing your progress. Think of it as risk management for your personal growth. For example, if you're aiming to learn a new language, consider the potential challenges—lack of time, difficulty with grammar, or limited access to language learning resources. Having a plan to address these challenges will help you stay on track even when faced with difficulties.

Equally important is setting realistic timelines. Avoid setting overly ambitious deadlines that will lead to pressure and stress. Give yourself ample time to achieve your goals, allowing for setbacks and unexpected delays. Overly tight deadlines can lead to hasty decisions and compromises on quality, ultimately undermining your efforts. For instance, if you're aiming to complete an online course, consider the time required for each module and allow sufficient time to absorb the material and complete assignments. Don't rush through the process simply to meet a deadline; focus on understanding and applying the knowledge.

Furthermore, it's vital to regularly assess your progress. Tracking your achievements, no matter how small, provides a sense of accomplishment and motivates you to continue. This regular evaluation also allows you to make adjustments as needed, ensuring that you're staying on track and making consistent progress. You might use a journal, a spreadsheet, or a dedicated app to track your progress. The key is to have a system that works for you and allows you to easily monitor your achievements and identify areas where improvements might be needed.

Self-compassion plays a crucial role in setting realistic goals. Remember to be kind to yourself throughout the process. Setbacks are inevitable, and it's essential to view them as learning opportunities rather than failures.

Instead of beating yourself up for not meeting a deadline or making a mistake, acknowledge the setback, learn from it, and adjust your approach accordingly. Celebrate your successes, no matter how small. Acknowledge your efforts and perseverance. This positive self-talk will build your resilience and keep you motivated.

Remember that progress, not perfection, is the goal. It's natural to strive for excellence, but aiming for perfection can be paralyzing. It often leads to procrastination and ultimately, prevents progress. Instead, focus on consistent improvement. Every small step you take, every obstacle you overcome, brings you closer to your goals. Recognize and celebrate these small wins to maintain momentum and stay motivated.

Visualization is also a powerful tool for setting realistic goals and expectations. Imagine yourself achieving your goals and experiencing the positive emotions associated with success. This mental rehearsal helps to build your self-confidence and reinforces your belief in your ability to achieve your objectives. Visualizing the process of achieving your goals—the steps involved, the challenges encountered, and the strategies used to overcome them—is equally beneficial.

Another crucial element is seeking support and accountability. Share your goals with trusted friends, family, or mentors who can provide encouragement and support. Consider joining a support group or finding an accountability partner who can help you stay motivated and on track. This social support network is invaluable in maintaining your commitment to your goals. Their encouragement can be crucial when you encounter setbacks or feel discouraged.

Finally, remember that setting realistic goals and expectations is an iterative process. As you progress, you may need to adjust your goals and timelines based on your experiences and newly gained insights. This flexibility and adaptability are key to long-term success. Your goals should evolve with you as you learn and grow. Regularly review your goals and adjust them as needed to keep them aligned with your current capabilities and aspirations.

The journey towards self-understanding and personal growth is a continuous process of learning, adapting, and refining your approach. Setting realistic goals and expectations is a crucial element of this process, providing a solid foundation for consistent progress and sustained motivation. Embrace the journey, celebrate your accomplishments, and remember that your potential is limitless. With realistic planning and consistent effort, you can achieve remarkable things.

Chapter 2: Embracing Your Productivity

Time Management Technics

Building upon the solid foundation of realistic goal setting, we now turn our attention to another critical pillar of productivity: time management. Effective time management isn't about cramming more into your day; it's about maximizing the impact of your time, ensuring you dedicate your energy to activities that truly align with your goals and contribute to your overall well-being. Many individuals fall into the trap of busywork, feeling perpetually overwhelmed yet achieving little of lasting significance. This section will equip you with practical strategies to reclaim control of your time and direct it towards activities that truly matter.

The first step in effective time management is understanding where your time currently goes. Before you can optimize your schedule, you need a clear picture of your current time allocation. This involves honest self-reflection and careful tracking. For a week, meticulously record how you spend your time, categorizing activities into productive, unproductive, and essential tasks.

"Productive" tasks directly contribute to your goals, "unproductive" activities distract you from your objectives, and "essential" tasks are necessary for daily living (like eating, sleeping, and personal hygiene).

This exercise might reveal surprising patterns. You might find yourself spending far more time on social media than you initially realized, or that unproductive meetings consume a significant portion of your workday. The goal isn't to beat yourself up for past time management shortcomings; it's about gaining valuable insight into your current habits to make informed changes. This awareness is the cornerstone of effective time management. Once you have a clear understanding of your time usage, you can start to identify areas for improvement.

Once you've mapped your current time usage, the next step involves prioritizing tasks. This is where the concept of the Eisenhower Matrix, also known as the Urgent-Important Matrix, comes into play. This matrix categorizes tasks based on their urgency and importance. Urgent tasks demand immediate attention, while important tasks contribute to your long-term goals. The matrix helps you prioritize tasks strategically, ensuring that you focus your time and energy on the most impactful activities.

Quadrant 1: Urgent and Important – These are crisis situations, deadlines you're about to miss, or pressing problems requiring immediate attention. While you can't entirely eliminate these tasks, the goal is to minimize their occurrence through proactive planning and effective delegation.

Quadrant 2: Important but Not Urgent – These are tasks that significantly contribute to your long-term goals but aren't pressing. This quadrant is where you should spend most of your time. These are activities that prevent future crises, such as planning, relationship building, exercise, and personal development. This is the area where proactive time management truly pays off.

Quadrant 3: Urgent but Not Important – These are interruptions, some meetings, some emails, and other time-consuming activities that often feel urgent but rarely contribute to your long-term goals. Learn to delegate these tasks or say "no" more often.

Quadrant 4: Neither Urgent nor Important – These are time-wasting activities such as excessive social media, mindless browsing, or unproductive meetings. These are activities you should eliminate or significantly reduce.

By consistently using the Eisenhower Matrix, you'll train yourself to focus your energy on what truly matters, preventing yourself from being overwhelmed by urgent but unimportant tasks. This proactive approach is key to long-term productivity and reduces stress significantly.

Time blocking is another powerful technique for effective time management. This method involves scheduling specific blocks of time for particular tasks or activities in your calendar. This creates structure and accountability, helping you stay focused and on track. When you schedule your tasks, be realistic about the time each will require.

It's better to overestimate than underestimate, creating buffer time to handle unexpected interruptions.

For instance, if you have a writing project, you might block out a 2-hour segment in the morning specifically for writing. During this time, you dedicate yourself solely to writing, avoiding distractions like emails or social media. The more consistently you use time blocking, the easier it becomes to integrate this technique into your daily routine.

Beyond time blocking, the Pomodoro Technique offers a structured approach to focused work. This technique involves working in focused bursts of *25* minutes (Pomodoros), followed by a *5*-minute break. After four Pomodoros, take a longer break of *15-20* minutes.

This method leverages the power of short, intense periods of focused work interspersed with regular breaks to maintain concentration and prevent burnout. Experiment with the length of your work and always feel free to break intervals to find what works best for you.

Another critical element of time management is learning to say "no." This often proves challenging, particularly for individuals who are naturally agreeable or feel pressured to overcommit. However, saying "no" to non-essential requests or tasks frees up valuable time and energy to focus on what truly matters. It's not about being selfish; it's about prioritizing your time and energy effectively.

Instead of feeling guilty about declining requests, above all just try to remember that it's a form of self-care, protecting your time and mental energy for the activities that truly align with your goals.

Effective delegation is also crucial. If you have the opportunity to delegate tasks, do so. This frees up your time to concentrate on higher-priority tasks that require your specific skills and expertise. This is especially relevant in the workplace, where effectively delegating responsibilities is crucial for efficient team management. Trust your colleagues and empower them to take on responsibilities, nurturing their growth while optimizing your own workflow.

Minimizing distractions is another essential aspect of effective time management.

Identify your common distractions—be it social media, email notifications, or interruptions from colleagues—and develop strategies to mitigate their impact. This might involve turning off notifications, using website blockers, or finding a quiet workspace where you can focus without interruptions.

Utilizing technology to your advantage can significantly improve time management. Calendar apps, task management tools, and productivity software can help you track your time, organize your tasks, and set reminders, facilitating efficient scheduling and reducing the likelihood of missed deadlines. Explore various applications and find those that best suit your individual needs and preferences. The key is to find a system that you'll consistently use, integrating technology into your workflow seamlessly.

Regularly reviewing and adjusting your time management strategies is crucial. Your needs and priorities might evolve over time, requiring you to refine your approach. Regularly evaluating your time management techniques, assessing their effectiveness, and making necessary adjustments ensures you remain on track and continue to optimize your productivity.

Finally, remember that effective time management is not about squeezing every second of your day into productive activities. It's about creating a sustainable system that prioritizes both productivity and well-being. Include time for relaxation, personal hobbies, and meaningful social connections. This ensures that your productivity efforts aren't detrimental to your overall happiness and mental health. Balance is key; a well-managed life is one that integrates productivity with rejuvenation. By diligently applying these time management techniques, you will transform your relationship with time, empowering yourself to achieve your goals and live a more fulfilling life.

Effective Organization Strategies

Building on the foundation of effective time management, we now delve into the crucial aspect of organization. A well-organized life is a productive life. Chaos and disarray are the enemies of efficiency; they sap your energy, breed procrastination, and ultimately hinder your ability to achieve your goals. Effective organization isn't about achieving a spotless, magazine-worthy home or office; it's about creating systems that support your workflow, minimizing wasted time and effort searching for misplaced items or struggling to locate necessary information. This section will provide you with practical strategies to organize your physical and digital spaces, streamline your workflows, and ultimately enhance your productivity.

The first step in effective organization is decluttering. This might seem daunting, but the payoff is significant. Decluttering isn't just about tidying up; it's about consciously evaluating each item and deciding if it adds value to your life. Start small, focusing on one area at a time. Begin with a drawer, a shelf, or a corner of a room. As you sort through your belongings, ask yourself these key questions: Have I used this in the past year? Does this item bring me joy or serve a practical purpose? If the answer to both questions is no, consider donating, selling, or discarding the item. Be ruthless in your decluttering efforts; holding onto unnecessary items only creates clutter and mental clutter, consuming valuable space and energy.

Decluttering your digital space is equally important. Our digital lives are often overflowing with files, emails, and applications we no longer need. Regularly delete unused files, unsubscribe from unnecessary email lists, and uninstall apps you haven't used in months. Organize your files into logical folders, using a consistent naming convention to facilitate easy retrieval. Consider cloud storage solutions to free up space on your devices and ensure data backup. Employing a strong search function for your files can significantly enhance your productivity.

Once you've decluttered, the next step is to establish clear systems for organizing the items you've retained. This involves creating designated spaces for everything, ensuring that each item has a home. For physical items, this might involve utilizing storage containers, drawers, shelves, and other organizational tools. Labeling containers is crucial for quick and easy retrieval. In your home, consider establishing designated zones for specific items, such as a mail station, a charging station, or a designated area for keys and wallets. These seemingly small measures significantly reduce time wasted searching for lost items.

For digital organization, utilize folders, tags, and other organizational tools provided by your operating system and applications. Consider using a cloud-based storage solution that allows you to access your files from multiple devices. Employ a consistent filing system that is intuitive and easy to follow. Utilize the search function of your files to optimize retrieval efficiency.

The Pareto Principle, also known as the *80/20* rule, can be a valuable tool in organizing your time and tasks. This principle suggests that *80%* of your results come from *20%* of your efforts. Identifying that crucial *20%* and prioritizing those tasks will drastically improve your productivity. It is about identifying your most important activities and focusing your energy and resources on them. This may mean delegating or outsourcing less critical tasks, or simply learning to say no to less important requests. By focusing on the vital few, you can achieve significant progress without feeling overwhelmed.

Another effective organizational technique is the "two-minute rule." If a task takes less than two minutes, do it immediately. This prevents small tasks from accumulating and becoming overwhelming. Answering a quick email, washing a single dish, or making your bed are all examples of tasks that can be completed in under two minutes.

Tackling these small tasks promptly prevents them from piling up and creating unnecessary stress.

Batching similar tasks is another powerful way to enhance efficiency. Instead of switching between various tasks throughout the day, group similar activities together. For example, respond to emails all at once, rather than checking your inbox intermittently. Complete all your phone calls in one block of time, and perform your household chores in a dedicated session.

This minimizes context switching and improves your overall focus.

Prioritization techniques, such as the Eisenhower Matrix (discussed previously), remain crucial in conjunction with organizational strategies. By prioritizing your tasks based on urgency and importance, you allocate your time and energy to the most impactful activities, making the most of your organized systems. Organizing your environment without a sound prioritization strategy is like arranging deck chairs on the

Titanic; it might look nice, but it ultimately fails to address the core challenges.

Beyond the individual tasks and projects, think about broader organizational strategies for your life. Creating a master to-do list, a comprehensive calendar, or a project management system can provide a holistic view of your commitments and responsibilities. This central repository allows you to track deadlines, progress, and upcoming events, preventing you from feeling overwhelmed or missing critical milestones. Regularly reviewing and updating these central systems is crucial for their effectiveness.

Developing effective habits is essential for maintaining organization. Establish a consistent routine for tidying your workspace, managing your emails, and tackling your tasks. Regular decluttering sessions, even if brief, prevent the accumulation of clutter. This consistent approach transforms organization from an occasional chore into an ingrained habit, seamlessly integrating into your daily life.

Regularly reviewing your organizational systems is crucial for ongoing success. Your needs and priorities might evolve over time, requiring you to adapt your strategies. Don't be afraid to experiment with different methods, finding what works best for your unique personality and workflow. The goal is to create a sustainable system that supports your productivity without adding undue stress or complexity. Organization should be a tool for empowerment, not a source of additional burden. By consistently applying these strategies, you can create an organized environment that promotes efficiency, reduces stress, and unlocks your full potential. The result is not simply a cleaner desk or a more tidy home; it's a more focused mind, greater clarity, and ultimately, a more productive and fulfilling life. Remember, effective organization is a journey, not a destination. Continuous refinement and adaptation are key to maintaining a streamlined and productive lifestyle. Embrace the process, and you will reap the rewards of a life well-organized and a mind well-focused.

Minimizing Distractions and Procrastination

Building upon the principles of effective organization, we now address the often-overlooked yet critically important aspects of minimizing distractions and conquering procrastination. These two insidious enemies of productivity can derail even the most meticulously planned schedules and organized environments. Understanding their mechanisms and developing strategies to mitigate their impact is paramount to achieving sustainable high levels of productivity.

Distractions are pervasive in our modern world. The constant barrage of notifications from our smartphones, the tempting allure of social media, the interruptions from colleagues or family members – these all chip away at our focus and disrupt our workflow. Procrastination, on the other hand, is a more insidious foe, often rooted in fear, perfectionism, or a lack of clarity about the task at hand. It's the insidious voice whispering, "Just five more minutes," that ultimately leads to missed deadlines and a sense of overwhelm.

Let's first tackle distractions. The key to minimizing their impact lies in cultivating a mindful awareness of your environment and your attention. Start by identifying your most common distractions. Is it the constant buzzing of your phone? The incessant chatter of your colleagues? The lure of browsing social media? Once you've pinpointed the culprits, you can begin to develop strategies to mitigate their effects.

One powerful technique is to create a dedicated workspace free from distractions. This might involve finding a quiet corner of your home or office, utilizing noise-canceling headphones, or simply turning off all notifications on your electronic devices. Consider using website blockers or apps that limit your access to distracting websites or applications during work hours. The goal is to create a sanctuary of focus, a space where you can immerse yourself in your work without interruption.

Beyond the physical environment, consider your mental state. Mindfulness practices, such as meditation or deep breathing exercises, can significantly enhance your ability to focus and resist distractions. These practices help to cultivate a greater awareness of your thoughts and feelings, allowing you to gently redirect your attention when it wanders. Regular breaks are also crucial for maintaining focus. Short, frequent breaks, rather than infrequent long ones, can help to prevent mental fatigue and improve your overall productivity. Use these breaks mindfully – engage in activities that are restorative and rejuvenating, such as stretching, going for a short walk, or listening to calming music.

Now let's address the issue of procrastination. Procrastination is rarely about laziness; it's often a symptom of underlying anxieties, fears, or a lack of clarity about the task at hand. Understanding the root cause of your procrastination is the first step in overcoming it. Are you afraid of failure? Do you feel overwhelmed by the sheer size of the task? Are you unclear about what's expected of you? Once you identify the underlying issue, you can begin to develop strategies to address it.

Breaking down large tasks into smaller, more manageable steps is a highly effective strategy for overcoming procrastination. A daunting project can feel paralyzing, but breaking it into smaller, more achievable chunks makes it seem less overwhelming. Create a detailed plan outlining each step involved, and celebrate your progress as you complete each step.

This approach not only helps to overcome procrastination but also provides a sense of accomplishment and momentum.

The Pomodoro Technique, a time management method involving *25*-minute focused work intervals followed by *5*-minute breaks, is another excellent tool for combating procrastination.

This structured approach helps to maintain focus and provides regular opportunities for rest, preventing burnout and maintaining motivation.

The short, focused work intervals make the task seem less daunting, and the regular breaks provide a much-needed mental reset.

Setting realistic goals is also crucial for preventing procrastination. Avoid setting overly ambitious goals that are likely to lead to feelings of overwhelm and discouragement. Instead, focus on setting achievable goals that provide a sense of accomplishment and momentum. Celebrate your successes along the way to maintain motivation and prevent feelings of stagnation.

Visualizing success can be a surprisingly powerful tool for overcoming procrastination. Take some time to visualize yourself successfully completing the task, experiencing the sense of accomplishment and satisfaction. This mental exercise can help to boost your motivation and confidence, making the task seem less daunting.

Another powerful technique is to use the power of accountability. Sharing your goals and progress with a friend, family member, or mentor can provide a significant boost of motivation. Knowing that someone else is aware of your progress can help to keep you on track and prevent procrastination.

Alternatively, consider joining a support group or online community where you can connect with others who share similar goals.

Finally, remember that self-compassion is crucial for overcoming procrastination. Be kind to yourself; setbacks are inevitable. When you slip up, don't beat yourself up about it. Instead, acknowledge the setback, learn from it, and get back on track. Procrastination is a common human experience; don't let it define you. Embrace the challenges, learn from your mistakes, and celebrate your successes. By developing these strategies and practicing self-compassion, you can effectively minimize distractions and conquer procrastination, ultimately unlocking your full potential for productivity.

Beyond individual techniques, consider integrating technology strategically. Utilize productivity apps designed to help manage your time, tasks, and projects effectively. Many applications allow for task prioritization, setting deadlines, and tracking progress, making the process of managing your workload more efficient and less prone to procrastination. These tools can act as external accountability mechanisms, reinforcing your commitment to your goals.

However, remember that technology itself can be a source of distraction. Therefore, carefully curate the applications you use, ensuring they truly enhance your productivity rather than hindering it. Be mindful of notification settings, limiting them to only the essential updates to avoid constant interruptions.

A well-organized digital workspace, mirroring the principles of physical organization, is equally crucial for maintaining focus and minimizing distractions.

Furthermore, nurture a supportive environment. Communicate your need for focused time to family members and colleagues, setting clear boundaries to minimize interruptions. Explain that you're working towards a specific goal and require dedicated time for optimal concentration. This proactive communication fosters understanding and respect for your focused work periods, reducing unnecessary disruptions.

Finally, recognize that overcoming distractions and procrastination is an ongoing process, not a one-time fix. It requires consistent effort, self-awareness, and a willingness to adapt your strategies as needed. Regularly evaluate your progress, identifying what works best for you and adjusting your approach accordingly. Embrace the journey, celebrate your successes, and learn from your setbacks. Remember, the ultimate goal is to create a sustainable system that supports your productivity and well-being, allowing you to achieve your goals with focus, efficiency, and a sense of accomplishment.

Building Effective Habits

Building effective habits is the cornerstone of sustained productivity. It's not enough to simply understand the principles of organization and distraction management; we must translate that understanding into consistent action through the development of robust, positive habits. This involves a conscious and deliberate process of cultivating new behaviors and replacing unproductive ones. The journey involves understanding the science behind habit formation, choosing the right habits, and implementing strategies for consistent execution and maintenance.

The power of habit lies in its automaticity. Once a behavior becomes habitual, it requires significantly less mental energy to execute. This frees up cognitive resources for more complex tasks and decision-making, leading to increased efficiency and productivity. However, the formation of beneficial habits isn't a passive process; it requires conscious effort, patience, and a structured approach.

Understanding the habit loop is crucial. This loop consists of three key elements: the cue, the routine, and the reward. The cue is the trigger that initiates the behavior; it could be a specific time of day, a location, a feeling, or even the completion of another task. The routine is the actual behavior itself – the action you perform. The reward is the positive reinforcement that strengthens the habit loop. It could be a feeling of satisfaction, a sense of accomplishment, or even a tangible reward.

To build effective habits, we must carefully design each component of the habit loop. For example, if you want to establish the habit of exercising regularly, you might choose a specific time (cue), such as 7 AM every morning, go to the gym (routine), and then reward yourself with a healthy smoothie and a feeling of accomplishment (reward). The key is to make the cue clear, the routine easy, and the reward satisfying.

Start small and build gradually. Trying to overhaul your entire life overnight is a recipe for failure. Instead, focus on building one new habit at a time. Choose a single, achievable goal, and meticulously design the habit loop to maximize your chances of success. Once you've successfully integrated that habit into your routine, you can gradually add more. This incremental approach allows for sustainable progress and prevents feelings of overwhelm.

Make it easy to succeed. One of the biggest mistakes people make when trying to build new habits is making them too difficult. The easier it is to perform the desired behavior, the more likely you are to stick with it. For instance, if your goal is to read more, keep a book by your bedside table, making it readily accessible. If you want to drink more water, keep a water bottle with you at all times. Remove any obstacles or barriers that might hinder your progress.

Track your progress. Keeping track of your progress is crucial for maintaining motivation and staying on track. Use a journal, a calendar, or a habit-tracking app to record your progress. Seeing your consistent effort will reinforce your positive behavior and provide a sense of accomplishment. This visual representation of your commitment can serve as a powerful motivator. Highlighting streaks of success can help you stay motivated through temporary setbacks.

Don't break the chain. The concept of "don't break the chain" is a powerful strategy for maintaining consistency. Visualize your habit as a chain, and each successful day as a link in the chain. Your goal is to keep the chain unbroken for as long as possible. Even if you miss a day, don't let it derail your progress. Simply pick up where you left off and keep going. The focus should be on consistency rather than perfection.

Find an accountability partner. Sharing your goals and progress with someone else can significantly increase your chances of success. An accountability partner can provide support, encouragement, and motivation. They can also help you stay accountable and on track when you feel like giving up. The act of sharing your intention creates a sense of responsibility and reinforces your commitment.

Reward yourself. Celebrate your successes along the way. This isn't about indulging in unhealthy habits, but rather about acknowledging your hard work and dedication.

A small reward, such as a relaxing bath or a favorite treat, can serve as a powerful motivator and reinforce positive behavior. The key is to choose rewards that are aligned with your overall goals and values.

Embrace flexibility and self-compassion. Building effective habits is a journey, not a destination. There will be setbacks along the way. Don't get discouraged if you miss a day or experience a temporary lapse in your routine. The most important thing is to learn from your mistakes and keep moving forward. Self-compassion is crucial – be kind to yourself, forgive yourself for occasional slip-ups, and focus on progress, not perfection.

Habit stacking is another powerful technique. This involves linking a new habit to an existing one. For example, you might decide to meditate for five minutes after you brush your teeth in the morning. This approach leverages the power of existing habits to establish new ones more easily. The familiar routine acts as a trigger for the new habit, making it more likely to stick.

Habit shifting involves identifying and replacing unproductive habits with productive ones. This requires identifying the underlying needs the unproductive habit fulfills. For example, if you frequently scroll through social media when feeling stressed, you might replace this habit with a healthier coping mechanism, such as meditation or exercise. Addressing the root cause helps create a sustainable shift.

Environmental design plays a vital role in habit formation. Restructure your environment to support your goals. If you want to read more, keep books readily available. If you want to eat healthier, keep healthy snacks visible and unhealthy snacks out of sight. The environment should make it easy to engage in productive behaviors and difficult to engage in unproductive ones.

Time blocking is a powerful technique to build habits tied to specific times. Schedule dedicated time slots for your new habit in your daily planner. Treating your habit like an important appointment ensures it receives the necessary attention and commitment. This is especially beneficial for habits that require concentration or specific time allocation.

Finally, remember that building effective habits is a marathon, not a sprint. It takes time, effort, and consistent dedication. But the rewards are well worth it. By developing a strong foundation of positive habits, you'll lay the groundwork for sustained productivity, greater self-discipline, and a more fulfilling life. Consistent effort, coupled with self-awareness, strategic planning and self-compassion, will ultimately lead to a life marked by increased efficiency and a profound sense of accomplishment.

Leveraging Technology for Productivity

Harnessing technology's power effectively is no longer a luxury; it's a necessity for maximizing productivity in today's fast-paced world. But simply owning the latest gadgets isn't enough. The key lies in understanding how to leverage technology strategically, turning potential distractions into powerful productivity tools. This requires a mindful approach, integrating technology into your workflow seamlessly and consciously avoiding its pitfalls.

One of the most significant advancements in productivity technology is the rise of project management tools. These applications provide a centralized hub for organizing tasks, setting deadlines, tracking progress, and collaborating with team members. Tools like Asana, Trello, Monday.com, and even simpler options like Google Tasks or Microsoft To Do can drastically improve workflow efficiency. The core benefit lies in their ability to visualize projects, break them into smaller manageable components, and provide a clear overview of what needs to be accomplished and when.

Experiment with different platforms to discover which best suits your individual working style and project needs.

Consider the nuances of each tool. Asana excels with complex projects requiring detailed task breakdowns and subtasks, while Trello's Kanban board system is visually appealing and particularly effective for visualizing workflow stages. Monday.com offers a high degree of customization and automation, suitable for larger teams and multifaceted projects. Google Tasks and Microsoft To Do, while simpler, are ideal for managing personal tasks and maintaining a clean, organized to-do list. The choice depends on your specific needs, team size, and project complexity.

Beyond project management, time-tracking apps have proven incredibly valuable for understanding where time is actually spent. Applications such as Toggl Track, RescueTime, and Clockify offer detailed insights into daily activities, identifying time sinks and areas for improvement. This self-awareness is crucial for optimizing workflow. Many of these apps integrate directly with project management tools, allowing for seamless tracking of time spent on individual tasks. Analyzing this data allows for a more realistic assessment of work capacity, enabling better project planning and preventing overcommitment.

You may discover that certain tasks consume significantly more time than anticipated, prompting a reassessment of your approach or delegation of tasks to others.

Effective communication is another area where technology plays a crucial role. Tools like Slack, Microsoft Teams, and Zoom facilitate seamless collaboration, reducing the time wasted on email chains and improving responsiveness. These platforms allow for instant messaging, file sharing, video conferencing, and project-based chat rooms, enhancing team dynamics and collaboration. The ability to quickly share updates, answer questions, and brainstorm ideas in real-time contributes significantly to productivity. However, mindful usage is essential. Avoid excessive notifications and schedule dedicated time slots for communication to prevent constant interruptions.

Email management is a perennial challenge for many. Developing a strategic approach to email is crucial. Consider setting aside specific times during the day to address emails, rather than constantly checking your inbox. Use filters and labels to organize emails, and prioritize tasks accordingly. Unsubscribing from unnecessary mailing lists significantly reduces clutter and frees up valuable time. Tools such as Sanebox or Mailstrom can automate much of this process, filtering out irrelevant emails and prioritizing important messages. By consciously managing email, rather than allowing it to control your schedule, you reclaim significant time for focused work.

Note-taking apps are another vital productivity tool. Instead of relying on scattered pieces of paper, applications such as Evernote, OneNote, or Notion provide a centralized repository for ideas, notes, research, and project plans. These apps often include features such as tagging, searching, and cross-referencing, making it easy to find and access information quickly.

Moreover, these platforms sometimes may seamlessly integrate with other productivity apps, strengthening the overall ecosystem of your workflow. The ability to quickly reference previous notes, research, and meeting minutes can save significant time and possibly mental energy.

The use of automation tools is becoming increasingly important. Services such as Zapier and IFTTT allow you to connect different applications and automate repetitive tasks, freeing up your time for more strategic work. For instance, you could automatically save emails to a specific folder, add new tasks to your project management tool, or send notifications based on specific triggers. By automating these mundane tasks, you significantly increase your efficiency and allow your mental energy to be directed towards more creative and complex undertakings.

However, alongside these technological aids, it is crucial to recognize the potential for distraction. Social media, constant email alerts, and the endless stream of notifications can quickly derail focus. Employ strategies to manage these distractions. This includes utilizing website blockers, scheduling social media breaks, turning off notifications, and creating dedicated workspaces free from distractions. Mindful technology usage involves consciously controlling the technology, rather than allowing the technology to control you.

The aim is to integrate technology seamlessly into your productive flow, rather than letting it become a constant source of interruption and mental clutter.

Moreover, remember that technology is a tool, not a solution. It's a means to an end, not an end in itself. Over-reliance on technology can lead to decreased critical thinking skills and an inability to work effectively offline. Maintaining a healthy balance between technological dependence and independent thinking is vital. Ensure you develop robust strategies for managing your technological consumption, setting boundaries, and prioritizing offline tasks as needed.

Finally, the key to leveraging technology for productivity lies in deliberate intention and consistent practice. Experiment with different tools and strategies to discover what works best for your individual work style and preferences. Regularly review your workflows, analyze your usage patterns, and adjust your approach as needed. The journey to maximizing productivity with technology is an ongoing process of refinement and adaptation, requiring constant awareness and adjustment. By thoughtfully integrating technology into your workflow and cultivating mindful usage habits, you can transform potential distractions into powerful tools for achieving your goals and enhancing your overall productivity.

Chapter 3: Mastering Your Social Interactions

Improving Communication Skills

Building upon our exploration of harnessing technology for productivity, we now turn our attention to another crucial aspect of maximizing your potential: mastering your social interactions. Effective communication is the cornerstone of strong relationships, both personal and professional. It's the bridge that connects us, enabling collaboration, understanding, and mutual respect. In today's interconnected world, where success hinges on teamwork and collaboration, honing your communication skills is no longer optional; it's essential.

Improving communication isn't simply about speaking eloquently; it's a multifaceted skill encompassing active listening, clear articulation, empathy, and nonverbal cues. Let's delve into practical strategies to elevate your communication prowess and foster deeper, more meaningful connections.

Active Listening: The Foundation of Effective Communication

Many believe communication is primarily about speaking, but true mastery lies in active listening. Active listening isn't passively hearing words; it's engaging fully with the speaker, understanding their message, and responding thoughtfully. It requires attentiveness, empathy, and a genuine desire to comprehend the other person's perspective.

Several techniques enhance active listening. First, eliminate distractions. Put away your phone, turn off the television, and focus entirely on the speaker. Maintain eye contact, demonstrating your engagement and respect. This nonverbal cue signals your undivided attention. Second, pay attention not only to the words but also to the speaker's tone, body language, and emotions. Often, nonverbal cues convey as much, if not more, than spoken words. A subtle shift in posture, a change in tone, or a fleeting facial expression can reveal underlying emotions or unspoken concerns.

Third, practice paraphrasing to ensure comprehension. Occasionally summarize the speaker's points in your own words, confirming your understanding and giving the speaker an opportunity to clarify any misunderstandings. This shows that you are actively processing their message and seeking clarity. For example, instead of simply saying "Okay," you might respond, "So, if I understand correctly, you're saying that the project deadline is causing you stress because of X and Y?" This not only demonstrates your attentiveness but can also open up a dialogue for further clarification and problem-solving.

Fourth, ask clarifying questions. Don't hesitate to ask questions to gain a deeper understanding of the speaker's perspective. This shows genuine interest and encourages further dialogue. Open-ended questions, starting with "how," "why," or "what," stimulate more detailed responses than simple yes-or-no questions.

For instance, instead of asking, "Did you enjoy the meeting?", try asking, "What were your key takeaways from the meeting?" The latter encourages a more thoughtful and appropriate informative response.

Finally, resist the urge to interrupt or formulate your response while the speaker is still talking. Give the speaker your full attention, allowing them to complete their thoughts before you respond. Interrupting not only disrupts the flow of conversation but also demonstrates a lack of respect for the speaker's perspective.

Clear and Concise Articulation: Getting Your Message Across

Once you've mastered active listening, the next step is to articulate your own thoughts and ideas clearly and concisely. This involves more than just choosing the right words; it's about structuring your message logically, using appropriate language, and ensuring your message is easily understood.

Start by organizing your thoughts before speaking. Consider what you want to convey and structure your message logically, progressing from point to point. This ensures your message is clear, coherent, and easy to follow. Use simple, straightforward language, avoiding jargon or technical terms that the listener may not understand. Tailor your language to your audience; a technical presentation to engineers will require a different vocabulary than a casual conversation with friends.

Pay attention to your tone of voice. A confident, even tone conveys clarity and authority, while a hesitant or uncertain tone can undermine your message. Practice speaking slowly and deliberately, pausing to allow your listener to process the information. Avoid using filler words like "um," "uh," or "like," which can detract from the clarity of your message. Practice speaking in front of a mirror or recording yourself to identify areas for improvement.

Employ storytelling to make your message more engaging. Humans are naturally drawn to stories; they provide a framework for understanding complex ideas and making them more relatable. When presenting information, consider weaving in relevant anecdotes or personal experiences to make your message more memorable and impactful. For instance, if you are explaining the importance of time management, sharing a personal story about how poor time management negatively impacted a project can be more effective than simply stating the importance of time management.

Nonverbal communication also plays a crucial role in clear articulation. Maintain eye contact, use appropriate gestures, and vary your tone to keep the conversation engaging. Be mindful of your body language; crossed arms or fidgeting can convey disinterest or nervousness. Your body language should complement and enhance your spoken words, reinforcing your message and creating a connection with your listener.

Empathy and Emotional Intelligence: Connecting on a Deeper Level

Effective communication transcends the mere exchange of information; it involves connecting with the other person on an emotional level. This requires empathy, the ability to understand and share the feelings of another person. Developing emotional intelligence, the ability to recognize, understand, and manage your own emotions and the emotions of others, is essential for fostering strong relationships and effective communication.

Practice putting yourself in the other person's shoes. Try to understand their perspective, their motivations, and their feelings, even if you don't agree with their point of view. This doesn't mean you have to agree with them; it simply means you are striving to understand their perspective. Acknowledge their feelings, even if you don't fully comprehend them. A simple statement like, "I understand you're feeling frustrated," can go a long way in validating the other person's emotions and building rapport.

Active listening is crucial for developing empathy. By attentively listening to the other person, you gain valuable insights into their emotional state and their underlying concerns. Pay attention to their nonverbal cues, which often reveal more than their spoken words. Observe their tone of voice, body language, and facial expressions to gauge their emotions.

Practice expressing empathy both verbally and nonverbally. Use empathetic language, such as "I understand," "I can see why you feel that way," or "I'm sorry you're going through this." Your body language should also reflect empathy; maintain eye contact, offer a comforting touch (if appropriate), and use open and inviting posture. Avoid interrupting or dismissing their feelings.

Develop self-awareness. Understanding your own emotions and how they impact your communication is crucial. If you are feeling angry, stressed, or overwhelmed, it will likely affect your communication style. Take time to manage your own emotions before engaging in a conversation. Try practicing some mindfulness techniques to help regulate your emotional responses and to improve your ability to truly remain calm and collected all while under pressure.

Nonverbal Communication: The Unspoken Language

Nonverbal communication encompasses all forms of communication that do not involve spoken words. This includes body language, facial expressions, tone of voice, eye contact, and personal space. Nonverbal cues often convey more than spoken words, influencing how your message is perceived and impacting the dynamics of the interaction.

Body language speaks volumes. Your posture, gestures, and facial expressions communicate your confidence, attitude, and emotional state. Open and relaxed body language, such as uncrossed arms and a relaxed posture, conveys approachability and openness. Closed-off body language, such as crossed arms and a tense posture, can convey defensiveness or disinterest. Be mindful of your posture and gestures to ensure they align with your message.

Eye contact is another vital aspect of nonverbal communication. Maintaining appropriate eye contact demonstrates engagement, confidence, and respect. Avoid staring intensely, which can be perceived as aggressive, or avoiding eye contact altogether, which can convey disinterest or dishonesty. Strive for a natural and comfortable level of eye contact that reflects genuine engagement.

Tone of voice plays a crucial role in how your message is interpreted. A warm and friendly tone conveys approachability and builds rapport, while a harsh or aggressive tone can be off-putting and damage the relationship. Practice modulating your tone to reflect the context of the conversation and the emotions you are conveying.

Personal space is another nonverbal cue to be mindful of. Respect the other person's personal space; avoid getting too close or too far away. The appropriate distance varies depending on cultural norms and the relationship between the individuals involved. Be sensitive to the other person's comfort level and adjust your distance accordingly. Understanding and effectively using these nonverbal cues can significantly enhance your communication skills and foster more meaningful connections.

By diligently practicing and integrating these strategies into your daily interactions, you will not only improve your communication skills but also cultivate stronger, more fulfilling relationships, both personally and professionally. Remember, effective communication is an ongoing journey of learning and self-improvement, and the rewards are immeasurable.

Building and Maintaining Healthy Relationships

Building and maintaining healthy relationships are crucial for overall well-being. Strong relationships provide support, belonging, and a sense of purpose, contributing significantly to happiness and life satisfaction. However, nurturing these relationships requires effort, understanding, and a willingness to invest time and energy. This section explores practical strategies to build and maintain healthy relationships, focusing on communication, empathy, and conflict resolution.

Communication: The Bedrock of Connection

Effective communication is the cornerstone of any healthy relationship. It's not just about what you say, but how you say it, and how you listen. Misunderstandings often stem from poor communication, leading to conflict and resentment. Open and honest communication, characterized by clear expression of thoughts and feelings, active listening, and mutual respect, is paramount.

To foster open communication, make a conscious effort to express your needs and feelings directly, using "I" statements to avoid blaming or accusing. For example, instead of saying "You always leave the dishes dirty," try "I feel frustrated when I see dirty dishes left in the sink." This approach focuses on your feelings rather than placing blame on the other person, making the message more receptive.

Active listening, as previously discussed, is equally vital. Truly hearing what the other person is saying, both verbally and nonverbally, shows respect and understanding. Pay close attention to their body language, tone of voice, and facial expressions. Ask clarifying questions to ensure you understand their perspective completely. Reflect back what you've heard to confirm your understanding and show that you're engaged. For example, you might say, "So, it sounds like you're feeling overwhelmed by the workload and need some support."

Beyond words, nonverbal cues play a significant role. Maintaining eye contact, using appropriate body language (open posture, relaxed facial expressions), and being mindful of your tone of voice all contribute to a positive and receptive communication environment. Avoid interrupting, dismissive behavior, or minimizing the other person's feelings.

Empathy: Walking in Another's Shoes

Empathy, the ability to understand and share the feelings of another person, is a powerful tool in building and maintaining strong relationships. It allows you to connect with others on a deeper level, fostering trust and strengthening bonds. To cultivate empathy, practice actively trying to understand the other person's perspective, even if you don't agree with their viewpoint.

Imagine yourself in their situation; consider their experiences, their beliefs, and the factors influencing their behavior. Ask questions to explore their feelings and experiences. Avoid judgment and resist the urge to immediately offer solutions. Sometimes, people just need to be heard and understood. Showing empathy might involve simply saying, "I can see why you're feeling this way," or "That sounds really challenging."

Expressing empathy involves validating the other person's emotions. Acknowledging their feelings, even if you don't share them, demonstrates your understanding and respect. For example, if a friend is expressing sadness over a loss, you might say, "I'm so sorry you're going through this. It must be incredibly painful."

This simple acknowledgment can make a world of difference. Avoid minimizing their feelings or offering unsolicited advice unless specifically asked for.

Conflict Resolution: Navigating Disagreements

Disagreements are inevitable in any relationship. How you handle these conflicts determines the health and longevity of the relationship. Effective conflict resolution involves approaching disagreements with a willingness to understand the other person's perspective, communicate openly and honestly, and find mutually acceptable solutions.

First, avoid escalating the conflict. Stay calm and composed, even when feeling frustrated or angry. Avoid personal attacks or accusatory language. Focus on the issue at hand, rather than resorting to character assassination or bringing up past grievances. Remember, the goal is to resolve the conflict, not to "win" an argument.

Second, actively listen to the other person's perspective. Try to understand their point of view, even if you don't agree with it. Show empathy by acknowledging their feelings and validating their experience. Ask clarifying questions to ensure you understand their concerns thoroughly.

Third, work towards finding a mutually acceptable solution. Compromise is key. Brainstorm different options, considering each person's needs and desires. Be willing to adjust your position to reach a compromise that works for everyone involved. It's also important to agree on a process for future conflict resolution – perhaps setting aside a specific time to discuss disagreements or agreeing on communication strategies to prevent escalation.

Fourth, after resolving the conflict, take time to reflect on the experience. What were the root causes of the disagreement? What could you have done differently? Learning from past conflicts can improve future interactions and strengthen the relationship.

Maintaining Healthy Boundaries

Setting and maintaining healthy boundaries is crucial for preserving your well-being and the health of your relationships. Boundaries are the limits you set to protect your physical, emotional, and mental health. They define what you're comfortable with and what you're not. Healthy boundaries ensure that your needs are met while respecting the needs of others.

Healthy boundaries aren't about being selfish; they are about self-respect. They allow you to maintain your identity and autonomy within the relationship. They also help prevent resentment and burnout. Clearly communicate your boundaries to others, explaining what you need and what you're not comfortable with. For example, you might establish boundaries around your time, personal space, or emotional availability.

Enforcing boundaries requires consistent communication and action. If someone crosses your boundaries, politely but firmly reassert them. Don't be afraid to say "no" when necessary. If you struggle to enforce your boundaries, it may be beneficial to seek professional support to develop strategies for effective communication and assertiveness.

Investing Time and Effort

Building and maintaining strong relationships requires consistent effort and investment of time and energy. Schedule regular time for connection – whether it's a weekly date night, a phone call, or simply a dedicated time for conversation.

These moments of connection strengthen the bond and foster intimacy.

Show appreciation and gratitude regularly. Express your love and appreciation for the other person's presence in your life. Small gestures of kindness, such as thoughtful gifts, acts of service, or words of encouragement, can go a long way in strengthening the relationship.

Seek professional help when needed. Relationship challenges are normal, but if you find yourselves consistently struggling, seeking guidance from a therapist or counselor can provide valuable tools and support for improving communication and resolving conflict. Remember that seeking help is a sign of strength and commitment to the relationship.

Building and maintaining healthy relationships is an ongoing process that requires constant nurturing and attention. By consistently practicing effective communication, cultivating empathy, resolving conflicts constructively, and setting healthy boundaries, you can cultivate strong, fulfilling relationships that enrich your life immeasurably. Remember, investing in these relationships is an investment in your overall well-being and happiness.

Overcoming Social Anxiety

Overcoming social anxiety often feels like navigating a minefield. Every interaction holds the potential for embarrassment, rejection, or judgment, leading many to withdraw and isolate themselves. But what if I told you that navigating these social situations doesn't have to be so terrifying? The good news is that social anxiety is manageable, and with the right tools and techniques, you can reclaim your social life and build meaningful connections.

The first step is understanding the root of your anxiety. Social anxiety, often stemming from a fear of negative evaluation, manifests differently in individuals. Some might experience intense physical symptoms like racing hearts, sweating, or trembling before or during social encounters. Others might struggle with overwhelming thoughts of inadequacy, self-consciousness, and a preoccupation with perceived flaws. It's crucial to identify your specific triggers and the patterns of thinking that fuel your anxiety. Keeping a journal documenting these experiences can offer valuable insights into your anxieties and how they manifest.

Note down situations that cause anxiety, the thoughts and feelings accompanying them, and the physical sensations you experience. This self-monitoring will be essential in developing personalized coping strategies.

Once you've identified your triggers, you can start to challenge the negative thoughts that perpetuate your social anxiety. Cognitive Behavioral Therapy (CBT) is a highly effective approach in this context. CBT focuses on identifying and modifying distorted thinking patterns that contribute to anxiety. For example, if you anticipate a

social gathering with the thought, "Everyone will judge me and think I'm boring," CBT encourages you to challenge this belief. Is it really likely that
everyone will judge you? What evidence supports this thought? What evidence contradicts it? Replacing catastrophic thoughts with more realistic and balanced ones is a crucial step towards managing your anxiety.

Exposure therapy is another powerful technique for overcoming social anxiety. This involves gradually exposing yourself to feared social situations, starting with less anxiety-provoking scenarios and gradually progressing to more challenging ones. This systematic desensitization helps to reduce the fear response associated with social interaction. For instance, if public speaking terrifies you, you might start by practicing in front of a mirror, then a small group of friends, and eventually working your way up to a larger audience.

The key is to do this gradually, ensuring that you don't overwhelm yourself at any stage. Celebrate each small victory; every successful step forward reinforces your sense of capability and confidence.

Mindfulness practices can be immensely beneficial in managing the physical and emotional symptoms of social anxiety. Techniques such as deep breathing exercises, meditation, and body scans help regulate your nervous system, reducing the intensity of anxiety symptoms.

When you find yourself feeling anxious, take a few deep breaths, focusing on the sensation of air entering and leaving your body. This simple act can help calm your racing heart and ease your physical tension. Regular mindfulness meditation can further enhance your ability to manage your emotional responses to social situations.

Social skills training can provide you with the tools to improve your communication and interaction skills. This might involve practicing active listening, assertive communication, and effective nonverbal communication. Role-playing exercises can be particularly helpful in building confidence and reducing anxiety associated with specific social interactions. Working with a therapist or coach in a safe and supportive environment will allow you to practice these skills and receive constructive feedback. Remember, these skills are learnable, and practicing them will increase your competence and confidence.

Building self-compassion is vital in the journey of overcoming social anxiety. Be kind to yourself, acknowledging that struggling with anxiety is not a sign of weakness. Recognize that everyone experiences moments of discomfort or self-doubt.

Instead of judging yourself harshly, treat yourself with the same kindness and understanding you would offer a friend that may be facing similar struggles. Self-compassion involves recognizing your imperfections and accepting your humanity.

Seeking professional help is a sign of strength, not weakness. A therapist can provide a safe space to explore the underlying causes of your social anxiety, develop personalized coping strategies, and provide support throughout your journey. Therapy can offer a tailored approach, focusing on your specific needs and challenges. Don't hesitate to reach out for professional support; it's an investment in your mental well-being and your future. Several therapeutic approaches, such as CBT, exposure therapy, and mindfulness-based therapies, have been proven effective in treating social anxiety disorder.

Remember, overcoming social anxiety is a journey, not a destination. There will be setbacks, and there will be moments of doubt. But with consistent effort, the right tools, and a supportive network, you can learn to manage your anxiety and build a more fulfilling social life. Celebrate your progress along the way. Each small step forward builds your confidence and strengthens your ability to navigate social interactions. Focus on building your resilience. Every time you face a challenging social situation and manage it, you build upon your capacity to handle future similar challenges with greater ease.

Your journey toward conquering social anxiety is a testament to your strength and determination; embrace the challenges and celebrate your victories.

Remember to practice self-care. Prioritizing your physical and mental well-being is crucial in managing anxiety. Ensure you're getting enough sleep, eating a healthy diet, exercising regularly, and engaging in activities you enjoy.

These practices will bolster your resilience and support your overall well-being, making you better equipped to manage anxiety-provoking situations.

Consider joining support groups. Connecting with others who share similar experiences can provide validation, support, and a sense of community. Sharing your struggles with others who understand can be incredibly helpful in reducing feelings of isolation and shame. These groups offer a safe space to learn from others' experiences and share coping strategies.

Consider the power of positive self-talk. Replace negative self-criticism with positive affirmations. Instead of focusing on your perceived flaws, highlight your strengths and accomplishments. Repeat positive affirmations daily to reinforce a more positive self-image and reduce self-doubt. For example, remind yourself, "I am capable," "I am worthy," and "I am confident." These affirmations, repeated regularly, can create a powerful shift in your self-perception.

Finally, remember that gradual progress is still progress. Don't get discouraged by setbacks. Acknowledge your efforts, celebrate your wins, and approach each new challenge with a renewed sense of determination. The journey to overcoming social anxiety is unique to you, and your progress is valuable regardless of the pace. Be patient with yourself, and celebrate each milestone along the way. You've got this.

Networking and Building Connections

Building a strong network isn't about collecting business cards; it's about cultivating genuine connections. It's about creating relationships built on mutual respect, understanding, and shared interests. This process, while initially daunting for someone struggling with social anxiety, becomes significantly easier when approached strategically and with self-compassion. Remember the progress you've already made in managing your anxiety; these skills will serve you well in building these connections.

Begin by identifying your existing network. Think beyond the immediate circle of family and close friends. Consider colleagues, former classmates, acquaintances from hobbies or interests, and even people you've met briefly but connected with on a personal level. Often, we underestimate the potential within our existing network. Reviewing your contacts and reflecting on past interactions can reveal hidden opportunities for deeper connections. Reach out to those you've lost touch with; a simple email or phone call expressing genuine interest in reconnecting can reignite dormant relationships.

Once you've assessed your current network, focus on expanding it strategically. This doesn't mean joining every group or attending every event. Instead, identify areas of genuine interest—professional development, hobbies, volunteering, or community involvement—and focus your efforts there. Participating in activities you enjoy will naturally lead to interactions with like-minded individuals, making the networking process more organic and less anxiety-inducing.

When attending networking events or joining groups, focus on quality over quantity. Don't feel pressured to meet as many people as possible. Instead, aim for meaningful interactions with a few individuals. Prepare a concise and engaging introduction about yourself, highlighting your interests and what you're looking for in a connection. Practice this introduction beforehand to boost your confidence. Avoid overly formal or rehearsed language; strive for genuine and conversational engagement.

Active listening is paramount in building connections. Pay close attention to what others say, ask thoughtful questions, and genuinely show interest in their experiences. People appreciate being heard and understood, and this genuine interest builds trust and rapport. Avoid interrupting and focus on fully absorbing what they are communicating, showing your sincere engagement through both verbal and nonverbal cues. Nodding, maintaining eye contact, and offering encouraging sounds like "uh-huh" or "I see" demonstrate active listening.

Remember the power of body language. Maintain open and welcoming posture, make eye contact (but avoid staring intensely), and offer a warm smile. These nonverbal cues signal approachability and confidence.

Consider your own comfort level; don't feel pressured to adopt a posture or style that feels unnatural. Authenticity is key; let your genuine personality shine through.

Following up after interactions is crucial in fostering new connections. Send a short email or message expressing your appreciation for the conversation and reiterating shared interests. This simple act reinforces the connection and indicates your genuine interest in maintaining the relationship. Avoid lengthy, impersonal emails; keep your message concise and personalized. Mention a specific aspect of your conversation to show that you were truly listening and engaged.

Online networking platforms can supplement your in-person efforts. LinkedIn, for example, provides a professional platform for connecting with colleagues and expanding your network. Engage in relevant groups, share insightful content, and participate in discussions to build your professional presence. Remember to maintain a professional profile and only connect with people you genuinely wish to engage with.

Don't feel pressured to connect with everyone; prioritize quality over quantity.

Don't be afraid to seek mentorship or guidance from individuals you admire. Mentorship relationships can provide invaluable support, advice, and direction. Express your admiration and interest in learning from their experience; most people are happy to share their knowledge and wisdom. Be prepared to articulate your goals and ambitions clearly. Show some genuine interest in their career path and be prepared to ask thoughtful questions.

Remember, networking is a two-way street. Be generous with your time and resources, offering support and assistance to others whenever possible. This reciprocal approach fosters stronger, more enduring relationships. Helping others not only strengthens your network, but it also boosts your own sense of self-worth and fulfillment. Look for opportunities to offer your skills, expertise, or simply a listening ear.

Building a strong network takes time and consistent effort. Don't be discouraged if you don't see immediate results. Focus on building genuine connections, rather than chasing superficial interactions. Celebrate small victories—a meaningful conversation, a new connection, or a mutually beneficial collaboration—as these successes reinforce your confidence and motivation. Remember to treat networking as an ongoing process, a continuous cycle of connecting, engaging, and nurturing relationships.

Overcoming the initial discomfort associated with networking requires self-compassion and a shift in perspective. Instead of viewing networking as a performance or a competition, view it as an opportunity to connect with like-minded individuals and share your passions. Embrace the imperfections; not every interaction will be perfect, and that's okay. Learn from each experience, and use it as an opportunity for growth.

Celebrate your wins, but don't be discouraged by setbacks; see them as valuable learning experiences. Remember to value the intrinsic rewards of building meaningful connections, and to focus on all the joys of engaging with people who might share your own passions.

When facing rejection or a lack of response, remember your self-worth is not contingent on others' responses. Not every connection will be successful, and that's simply a part of the process. Analyze interactions that didn't go as well as hoped to identify areas for improvement.

Did you feel rushed? Did you anticipate negative outcomes, hindering your ability to connect? Focus on building stronger skills that will enhance your ability to connect with people more successfully in the future. Always maintain a positive outlook, celebrate your strengths, and use any setbacks as opportunities for improvement and growth.

Networking extends beyond professional contexts. Building a strong social network enhances your overall well-being and provides support during challenging times. Engage in activities that nurture your personal interests, enabling you to meet new people with shared passions. Joining a book club, taking a dance class, volunteering for a charity, or participating in local community events can lead to meaningful friendships and strengthen your support system. These relationships offer not only companionship and shared experiences but also provide a sense of belonging and increased resilience.

Remember the importance of maintaining existing relationships. While building new connections is crucial, nurturing your existing relationships is equally vital. Stay in touch with friends and family; schedule regular social gatherings, offer support during challenging times, and celebrate their achievements. These steadfast relationships form the bedrock of your social support network, providing stability and emotional resilience. Nurturing these relationships helps prevent feelings of isolation and reinforces a sense of belonging.

Finally, consider the benefits of reciprocal relationships. These are connections built on mutual support and exchange. Offer your skills and time to others, and be open to receiving support in return. This balance is key to developing healthy, sustainable connections, and it provides a sense of reciprocity that strengthens the bond.

This mutually beneficial approach can potentially increase the likelihood of enduring healthy relationships and builds a deeper sense of trust and connection.

Remember, building a network is a journey, not a destination. Embrace the process, celebrate your successes, and learn from setbacks. The rewards of building strong, meaningful connections are immeasurable, providing not only professional opportunities, but also enriching personal relationships and fostering a stronger sense of belonging and overall well-being.

You have the power to create the network you envision; embrace the journey and watch your connections flourish.

Setting Boundaries in Relationships

Building healthy relationships requires more than just showing up; it necessitates establishing clear and consistent boundaries. This is crucial not only for protecting your emotional well-being but also for fostering respectful and mutually fulfilling connections. Without boundaries, you risk being taken advantage of, feeling resentful, and ultimately damaging the relationship itself. Setting boundaries is an act of self-respect and a demonstration of your understanding of your own needs and limitations.

The first step in setting boundaries is self-awareness. Truly understanding your own needs, preferences, and limits is fundamental. What situations or behaviors consistently drain your energy or compromise your well-being? What are your non-negotiables? Spend some time reflecting on past relationships and identifying patterns. Journaling can be a powerful tool for this self-reflection.

Write about past experiences where you felt taken advantage of, where your needs were disregarded, or where you compromised your values.

Analyzing these experiences will illuminate your personal boundaries and highlight recurring themes.

Once you've identified your personal boundaries, the next step involves clearly communicating them to others. This often requires overcoming the fear of conflict or rejection. Remember, expressing your needs isn't selfish; it's an essential component of healthy relationships. Clear communication is vital, so avoid ambiguity or passive-aggressive behavior. Be direct, assertive, and respectful in your communication. Use "*I*" statements to express your feelings and needs without blaming or accusing the other person. For instance, instead of saying "You always make me late," try, "When we're running late, it causes me stress."

Consider using the "broken record" technique, where you calmly and repeatedly restate your boundary even when faced with resistance or pushback. This technique is particularly useful when dealing with individuals who persistently try to cross your boundaries. For example, if a friend constantly calls you late at night disrupting your sleep, you can calmly and repeatedly say, "I appreciate you thinking of me, but I need to prioritize my sleep schedule, and I'm unable to answer calls after *10* pm."

Practicing your communication is essential. Role-playing with a trusted friend or therapist can help you feel more comfortable and confident in expressing your boundaries. The goal isn't to deliver a perfect performance; it's about feeling comfortable and authentic in your communication. Practice makes perfect, and the more you practice expressing your boundaries, the easier and more natural it will become.

Setting boundaries isn't a one-time event; it's an ongoing process. You may need to readjust your boundaries as your needs and priorities change, or as the dynamics of a relationship evolve. This is normal and reflects the dynamic nature of relationships. Be prepared to revisit and adjust your boundaries as needed to maintain a healthy balance. Regular self-reflection will help you stay attuned to your evolving needs and ensure your boundaries remain effective.

Enforcing your boundaries is equally crucial. This involves consistently upholding the boundaries you've established. If someone violates your boundary, you need to take appropriate action. This might involve calmly but firmly restating your boundary, setting consequences for future violations, or even temporarily or permanently distancing yourself from the individual. The specific action will depend on the nature of the violation and the relationship itself.

Consider creating a hierarchy of consequences. For example, a minor violation might warrant a gentle reminder, while a more serious violation might require more significant action, such as ending the interaction or limiting future contact. Consistency is key; be prepared to follow through on the consequences you've set. Inconsistent enforcement weakens your boundaries and undermines their effectiveness.

Remember that setting boundaries isn't about pushing people away; it's about creating space for healthy, reciprocal relationships. It's about protecting your energy and well-being so that you can contribute positively to your relationships. By setting boundaries, you're essentially saying, "I respect myself, and I expect to be respected in return." This empowers you to engage in relationships that are both fulfilling and supportive.

Setting boundaries can be particularly challenging in close relationships, like those with family members. Family dynamics can be complex and deeply ingrained. You may feel pressure to conform to established patterns or fear causing conflict. However, maintaining healthy boundaries within your family is crucial for both your well-being and the health of the relationship. Start small, focusing on less emotionally charged areas. Gradually work towards addressing more challenging aspects of your family relationships, always remembering that your boundaries are designed to protect your well-being.

In romantic relationships, boundaries are equally important. They ensure that each person's individual needs and autonomy are respected. Healthy romantic relationships are built on mutual respect, understanding, and the ability to communicate needs and limits effectively. Defining boundaries around personal space, time, finances, and emotional intimacy contributes to a healthy and balanced relationship, where each person feels valued and respected. It's about finding the sweet spot between intimacy and individuality.

One common challenge in setting boundaries is the fear of jeopardizing relationships. You may worry that being assertive will lead to conflict or rejection. However, healthy relationships can withstand boundary setting. In fact, clear boundaries often strengthen relationships by fostering respect, trust, and open communication. If a relationship cannot withstand healthy boundaries, then it may not be a healthy relationship to begin with.

Another challenge is the tendency towards people-pleasing. Some individuals prioritize the needs and desires of others above their own. This can stem from various factors, including low self-esteem, fear of rejection, or a deeply ingrained desire to be liked and accepted. Overcoming people-pleasing requires self-compassion, self-acceptance, and a conscious effort to shift your focus towards your own needs. Start by making small changes, gradually prioritizing your own needs and expressing your preferences more assertively.

Remember that setting boundaries is a skill that improves with practice. It's not about being perfect; it's about consistently working toward creating healthier, more fulfilling relationships. Expect setbacks along the way, and use these experiences as opportunities for learning and growth. Recognize that you are worthy of respect and healthy relationships, and that setting boundaries is a vital step in achieving both.

Consider seeking professional support if you struggle to set boundaries effectively. A therapist or counselor can provide guidance and support in identifying your needs, developing effective communication strategies, and overcoming any underlying issues that may be hindering your ability to establish and maintain healthy boundaries.

They can also offer tools and techniques to help you address the fear of conflict or rejection.

The ability to set and maintain boundaries is an essential life skill, impacting not only your relationships but also your overall well-being. By prioritizing your own needs and effectively communicating your limits, you create space for healthier, more fulfilling interactions and foster a stronger sense of self-respect and self-worth.

Remember, setting boundaries is an act of self-love and a crucial step towards building the life you want. It's an investment in your happiness and well-being, creating a space where you can thrive both personally and in your relationships.

The journey may have its challenges, but the rewards of creating healthier, more fulfilling connections are immeasurable.

Chapter 4: Achieving Your Goals and Aspirations

Goal Setting and Action Planning

Building upon the foundation of healthy boundaries, we now turn our attention to the crucial elements of goal setting and action planning. These are not merely abstract concepts; they are the practical tools that transform aspirations into tangible realities. Just as strong boundaries protect your emotional well-being, clear goals and effective action plans safeguard your progress toward a fulfilling life. Without them, even the most fervent desires can remain elusive, lost in a sea of unfocused effort.

Effective goal setting begins with self-reflection. What truly matters to you? What are your deepest values and aspirations? Consider your personal mission statement – the underlying purpose that guides your life choices. Reflect on past successes and failures. What patterns emerge? What strategies worked well, and what needs improvement? This introspective process lays the groundwork for setting goals that are both meaningful and attainable.

Avoid the trap of setting vague or overly ambitious goals. Instead, focus on specific, measurable, achievable, relevant, and time-bound (SMART) goals. For example, instead of aiming to "be healthier," define a SMART goal like "lose *10* pounds by incorporating *30* minutes of exercise daily and following a balanced diet for the next three months." The specificity ensures clarity, while the measurability allows for tracking progress and making necessary adjustments along the way. Achievability keeps you motivated by setting realistic targets, while relevance ensures alignment with your overall life goals. Finally, the time bound element provides a crucial deadline, preventing procrastination and maintaining momentum.

Break down large goals into smaller, manageable steps. This creates a sense of accomplishment as you complete each step, building momentum and confidence. Consider using a project management approach, breaking down your primary goal into phases, tasks, and sub-tasks. This methodical approach will help in creating a structured roadmap leading towards the achievement of your aspirations.

For example, if your primary goal is to write a book, you can break it down into phases such as research, outlining, writing chapters, editing, and publishing. Each of these phases will further be broken down into specific tasks, ensuring that the process is easily manageable and sustainable. Using digital tools or a physical planner will greatly assist in this task breakdown. Creating a visual representation, like a mind-map or Gantt chart, can help you visualize your progress and identify potential roadblocks.

Action planning is the bridge between goal setting and achievement. It involves outlining the specific steps required to reach your goals, setting deadlines for each step, and allocating the necessary resources. Consider various factors while creating your action plan. Your action plan shouldn't be rigid. Make it flexible and adaptable to respond to changes in your circumstances.

For instance, unexpected events can significantly affect the progress of your action plan. It's imperative to be prepared for such contingencies and have alternatives or backup plans in place.

Moreover, ensure that your action plan accounts for potential obstacles and challenges. Anticipating these roadblocks allows you to develop strategies to mitigate them proactively. It involves identifying potential difficulties that might hinder the progress of your goals and devising ways to overcome them. Developing contingency plans for anticipated challenges ensures that you remain on track even when facing unexpected hurdles.

Regularly review and revise your action plan. Life is dynamic, and your goals and circumstances may evolve over time. This requires a periodic review of your action plan, allowing for adjustments based on your progress and feedback. A regular review will help you stay on track, identify any emerging challenges and make the necessary adjustments. This adaptive approach ensures your plan remains relevant and effective throughout your journey.

Accountability is key to successful goal achievement. Consider sharing your goals with a trusted friend, family member, or mentor. Regular check-ins can provide support, encouragement, and feedback. Or consider joining a support group or online community focused on your specific goal. This shared journey can provide additional motivation and valuable insights. Accountability helps in maintaining focus and consistency, which is crucial for achieving long-term goals.

Celebrate your successes along the way. Acknowledge your accomplishments, no matter how small. This positive reinforcement strengthens your motivation and reinforces the belief in your ability to achieve your goals. Acknowledging and celebrating milestones will help in maintaining motivation and commitment, which is vital for long-term success.

Don't be afraid to adjust your goals or action plan as needed. This flexibility allows you to adapt to changing circumstances and maintain momentum. This flexibility ensures your plans remain relevant and effective in light of any unforeseen circumstances or challenges.

Remember, the journey toward achieving your goals is not always linear. There will be setbacks, challenges, and moments of doubt. But by maintaining a clear focus, a well-defined action plan, and a commitment to consistent effort, you can overcome these obstacles and ultimately reach your aspirations.

The process of goal-setting and action planning is a cyclical one. As you achieve your goals, you'll gain valuable insights into your strengths and weaknesses, informing the development of future goals and action plans. Each accomplishment builds upon the last, creating a positive feedback loop that propels you forward on your journey toward a more fulfilling and meaningful life.

Don't underestimate the power of visualization. Imagine yourself achieving your goals. Feel the emotions associated with success. This mental rehearsal can significantly enhance your motivation and commitment, bolstering your determination and perseverance. The power of visualization should never be underestimated.

Furthermore, consider the importance of self-compassion. There will be times when you falter or encounter setbacks. Practice self-forgiveness and learn from your mistakes. Treat yourself with the same kindness and understanding you would offer a close friend facing similar challenges. Self-compassion is not about self-indulgence; it's about nurturing yourself through difficult times and maintaining your emotional well-being throughout the process.

Finally, remember that achieving your goals is a personal journey. There is no one-size-fits-all approach. Experiment with different strategies, find what works best for you, and adapt your methods as needed. Trust in your ability to achieve your goals and celebrate each milestone along the way.

This personal journey requires patience, perseverance, and unwavering commitment. By embracing these principles and staying committed, you will pave the way toward a more fulfilled and meaningful life. The achievement of your goals is a testament to your determination and self-belief. Embrace the journey and enjoy the process of achieving your dreams.

The path may have its obstacles and challenges, but the rewards of perseverance and commitment are invaluable.

Overcoming Obstacles and Setbacks

Overcoming obstacles is an inevitable part of the journey towards achieving your goals. It's not a matter of if you'll encounter setbacks, but when. The key lies not in avoiding them altogether – that's often impossible – but in developing the resilience and strategies to navigate them effectively.

Start to think of obstacles as detours, not dead ends. They are opportunities for learning, growth, and a deeper understanding of your own capabilities.

One of the most common obstacles is procrastination. We all experience it; that nagging feeling that tells us to put things off until later. This often stems from fear of failure, feeling overwhelmed by the task at hand, or a lack of clarity on the next steps. To combat procrastination, break down large tasks into smaller, more manageable chunks.

This reduces the feeling of being overwhelmed and makes the task less daunting. Use time management techniques like the Pomodoro Technique, which involves working in focused bursts with short breaks in between. Reward yourself for completing smaller tasks to reinforce positive behavior and maintain motivation.

Perfectionism is another significant obstacle. While striving for excellence is commendable, perfectionism can be paralyzing. It can lead to analysis paralysis, where you spend so much time planning and perfecting that you never actually start. Remember that progress, not perfection, is the key. Embrace imperfection and learn from your mistakes. Focus on making progress, even if it's not perfect. Each step forward, no matter how small, contributes to your overall success. Celebrate small wins to boost your confidence and motivation.

Fear of failure is a powerful inhibitor. The fear of not meeting expectations, either your own or others', can prevent you from even attempting to pursue your goals. This fear can manifest in various ways: self-doubt, anxiety, and avoidance. To overcome this fear, challenge your negative self-talk. Identify and reframe your negative thoughts into more positive and realistic ones. Focus on the learning process and view setbacks as opportunities for growth. Remember that failure is not the opposite of success; it's a stepping stone towards it. Embrace the lessons learned from past failures and use them to inform your future endeavors.

Lack of support can also hinder your progress. While self-reliance is crucial, having a supportive network can make a significant difference. Surround yourself with positive and encouraging people who believe in your abilities and provide constructive feedback. This support system can offer encouragement, guidance, and accountability, helping you stay motivated and focused on your goals. Consider joining a support group or online community related to your goals, connecting with others who are pursuing similar aspirations. Sharing your experiences, challenges, and successes can provide valuable insights and mutual support.

Unexpected life events, such as illness, job loss, or family emergencies, can disrupt your plans and create significant setbacks. These are often unavoidable, but you can mitigate their impact by having a contingency plan. This plan should include identifying potential disruptions, developing alternative strategies, and having resources in place to help you navigate through unforeseen circumstances. Flexibility and adaptability are crucial in these situations. Be willing to adjust your goals and timelines as needed, recognizing that life often throws curveballs.

Burnout is another significant obstacle, especially when pursuing ambitious goals. Overworking can lead to exhaustion, demotivation, and a decreased ability to focus. Prevent burnout by prioritizing self-care. Ensure you get adequate rest, exercise regularly, eat a healthy diet, and engage in activities you enjoy. Schedule regular breaks to recharge and avoid overcommitting yourself. Learn to recognize the signs of burnout and take proactive steps to address them.

Financial constraints can also impede your progress, particularly if your goals require significant resources. Develop a realistic budget and explore ways to secure the necessary funds. This may involve seeking financial assistance, finding creative solutions, or adjusting your goals to align with your current financial situation. Remember, achieving your goals is a marathon, not a sprint. It's perfectly acceptable to adjust your timeline and approach based on your financial circumstances.

Maintaining momentum can be challenging, especially during periods of low energy or motivation. To overcome this, establish a consistent routine and stick to it as much as possible. Celebrate small wins to reinforce positive behavior and motivate you to continue your progress. Reflect on your progress regularly and adjust your strategy as needed. Remember your "why" – the reason behind your goals – to reignite your passion and commitment.

Self-doubt can creep in, undermining your confidence and belief in your abilities. Challenge negative self-talk and replace it with positive affirmations. Focus on your strengths and past successes. Remember that everyone experiences self-doubt, and it's a normal part of the journey. Cultivate self-compassion and treat yourself with kindness and understanding.

Finally, remember that overcoming obstacles requires perseverance and resilience. It's about maintaining a positive mindset, adapting to changing circumstances, and learning from your mistakes. Celebrate your achievements, no matter how small, and view setbacks as opportunities for growth. The journey towards achieving your goals is not always linear; it's often filled with twists, turns, and obstacles. But by embracing these challenges and developing the strategies to navigate them, you will not only reach your goals but also emerge stronger and more resilient. The journey itself will be transformative, shaping you into a more capable and confident individual. Believe in your ability to overcome any hurdle, and remember that the reward of achieving your aspirations far outweighs the challenges encountered along the way.

Maintaining Motivation and Momentum

Maintaining momentum is the lifeblood of achieving any goal, large or small. It's the consistent forward movement that separates dreams from reality. But maintaining that momentum isn't always easy. Life throws curveballs; fatigue sets in; doubt whispers insidious lies. This section will equip you with strategies to keep the fire burning brightly, even when the path gets rough.

One of the most effective techniques for sustaining motivation is the power of consistent action. Think of it like building muscle: you don't get biceps overnight; you need consistent exercise. Similarly, achieving your goals requires consistent effort, even in small doses. Instead of aiming for monumental leaps, focus on making small, incremental strides each day. Even 15 minutes of focused work on your goal is better than nothing. This small, consistent effort compounds over time, leading to significant progress. Establish a daily or weekly routine dedicated to your goal, treating it with the same importance as any other crucial appointment. This routine could involve setting aside specific times for working on your project, reviewing your progress, or engaging in activities that support your goal. The key is consistency, not perfection.

Another crucial element is the art of self-reward. Our brains are wired to respond positively to rewards. This isn't about indulging in excessive treats, but about acknowledging and appreciating your efforts. Each small victory deserves recognition. Did you finish that chapter of your book? Celebrate it! Did you complete a challenging task at work that contributes to your career aspirations? Reward yourself with something you enjoy, whether it's a relaxing bath, a walk in nature, or a delicious meal. These small rewards reinforce positive behavior and keep you motivated to continue your progress. Make sure your rewards align with your overall goals; a celebratory dessert might not be the best reward if your goal is weight loss, for example. Instead, find a reward that supports and celebrates your journey, perhaps a new fitness outfit or a massage.

Visualizing success is a surprisingly powerful motivator. Regularly picturing yourself achieving your goal, feeling the emotions associated with success, strengthens your commitment and belief in your capabilities. This mental rehearsal helps you stay focused on the positive outcome, boosting your confidence and perseverance. Take a few minutes each day to vividly imagine yourself achieving your goal. Engage all your senses:

what do you see, hear, smell, taste, and feel? The more vivid and detailed your visualization, the more effective it will be.

Tracking your progress is another vital component of maintaining momentum. This involves regularly monitoring your achievements, noting milestones reached, and analyzing areas where improvement is needed. Use a journal, a spreadsheet, or a dedicated app to track your progress. Seeing your progress visually can be incredibly motivating, offering tangible evidence of your efforts and success. Regularly reviewing your progress allows you to celebrate accomplishments and identify areas needing adjustment. This process reinforces positive behavior, motivating you to continue your journey. More importantly, it helps you stay accountable to yourself and your goals.

Regular reflection is essential for maintaining momentum. Take time to reflect on your progress, challenges, and successes. This process allows you to identify patterns, learn from mistakes, and adjust your strategies as needed. Ask yourself questions like: What progress have I made? What obstacles have

I encountered? What strategies have worked well? What adjustments do I need to make? This reflective process allows you to fine-tune your approach, ensuring you remain focused and on track. Don't be afraid to adjust your plan as you gain experience and discover what truly works best for you.

The importance of community cannot be overstated. Surrounding yourself with supportive individuals who believe in your abilities and provide constructive feedback is invaluable. This could involve joining a support group, connecting with mentors or coaches, or simply sharing your goals with trusted friends and family. Knowing you have people cheering you on can make a world of difference when motivation wanes. Sharing your experiences, challenges, and successes with others can provide valuable insights and mutual support, strengthening your resolve and reminding you that you are not alone on this journey. Their encouragement and understanding can be a powerful antidote to self-doubt and fatigue.

However, even with the best strategies, there will be times when motivation dips. This is perfectly normal. Don't beat yourself up over it. Instead, recognize that these are temporary setbacks. Take a break, recharge, and return to your goals with renewed energy. When motivation flags, reconnect with your "why." Remember the reasons behind your goals, the dreams that fueled your initial ambition. Rediscovering this passion will reignite your drive and commitment. Write your "why" down and keep it visible as a reminder.

Another key aspect of sustaining momentum is the ability to adapt. Life is unpredictable;

unexpected events can throw off even the best-laid plans. It's crucial to remain flexible and adaptable. When faced with unforeseen challenges, don't get discouraged; instead, reassess your goals and strategies. Are there alternative routes to achieving your objectives? Can you adjust your timeline or approach to account for the unexpected? Remember that progress, not perfection, is the key.

Finally, cultivate self-compassion. Be kind to yourself, especially during times of struggle. Remember that setbacks are part of the journey. Don't let occasional dips in motivation derail your progress. Forgive yourself for any slip-ups, learn from them, and move forward. Self-compassion is not about self-indulgence; it's about treating yourself with the same kindness and understanding you would offer a friend facing similar challenges. This inner support system will help you navigate the inevitable ups and downs of the journey. Remember that achieving your goals is a marathon, not a sprint. There will be moments of intense effort and moments of rest and reflection. Embrace the entire process, celebrating both the victories and the lessons learned from any setbacks. The journey itself is a testament to your resilience and commitment, shaping you into a stronger, more capable individual. The destination is important, but the transformation along the way is just as valuable.

Celebrating Success and Recognizing Progress

Celebrating successes, no matter how small, is crucial for maintaining momentum. It's a powerful positive feedback loop that reinforces the behaviors leading to progress.

Think about it: when you accomplish something, your brain releases dopamine, a neurotransmitter associated with pleasure and reward. This positive reinforcement makes you want to repeat the behavior that led to the success, creating a virtuous cycle of achievement.

The key here isn't just celebrating the grand finale, the ultimate achievement of your goal. It's about celebrating the journey, the smaller milestones along the way. Did you finally finish that daunting report at work? Did you manage to stick to your exercise routine for a whole week, even when you were tempted to skip a session? Did you complete a chapter of your novel, or learn five new vocabulary words in a foreign language? These might seem insignificant in the grand scheme of your overarching goals, but they are significant steps forward. Each deserves recognition and celebration.

How do you celebrate these smaller successes? The answer is highly personal. It depends on your personality, your preferences, and what brings you joy. Some people might prefer a quiet moment of self-reflection, acknowledging their accomplishment with a sense of pride and satisfaction. Others might find it more rewarding to share their success with loved ones, receiving their support and encouragement. Still others might choose to celebrate with a small, tangible reward, like a delicious treat, a relaxing bath, or a new book.

The effectiveness of a celebration isn't necessarily tied to the extravagance of the reward. A small act of self-care – a *15*-minute meditation session, listening to your favorite music, or a short walk in nature

– can be as effective as a lavish celebration. The key is to make the celebration meaningful and personal. It's about acknowledging your effort and progress, reinforcing the positive feelings associated with achievement.

Moreover, celebrating successes isn't just about feeling good; it's about learning. When you take time to acknowledge your wins, it allows you to reflect on what worked, what strategies were effective, and what you can replicate in the future. This reflective process strengthens your self-efficacy, that is, your belief in your own ability to succeed. When you consistently celebrate your successes, you build a stronger sense of confidence, resilience, and belief in your capabilities, fueling your motivation to keep going.

Recognizing progress goes hand-in-hand with celebrating successes. While celebrating focuses on the achievement, recognizing progress focuses on the journey itself. It's about acknowledging the incremental steps you've taken, even if you haven't yet reached the ultimate destination. This is particularly crucial when dealing with long-term goals that require sustained effort over an extended period. These are the goals that can often feel overwhelming, leading to discouragement and a sense of being stuck.

Progress recognition helps you maintain perspective, reminding you that you are, in fact, moving forward, even if the progress is subtle. Consider tracking your progress visually – using a progress chart, a calendar with checkmarks, or a journal detailing your daily efforts. The visual representation of your achievements can be incredibly motivating, offering tangible proof of your hard work and dedication. It helps to counteract any feelings of frustration or discouragement by showcasing the distance already covered.

This isn't about obsessing over minute details or constantly comparing yourself to others. It's about maintaining a balanced perspective, acknowledging both your successes and the areas where further effort is needed. Recognizing progress requires a shift in mindset, from focusing solely on the destination to appreciating the journey itself. It's about celebrating not just the arrival but the process of getting there, the growth and development that occur along the way.

This process involves regularly assessing your progress against your initial goals and objectives. This is an excellent time to review your strategies. What's working well? What needs improvement? Have external factors influenced your progress? Are your goals still relevant, or do they need adjusting in light of your experiences and newfound insights? This regular self-assessment is vital, allowing for course correction and ensuring that you're staying on track towards your desired outcomes.

For example, if your goal is to write a novel, regularly assessing your progress might involve tracking your word count, evaluating the plot development, and reflecting on the overall quality of your writing. If you're training for a marathon, you would track your running distances, times, and overall fitness level. If you're aiming to improve your financial situation, you would monitor your income, expenses, savings, and investment growth. In each instance, the key is to choose metrics that provide a clear and concise picture of your progress.

The importance of accurately assessing your progress cannot be overstated. It's about making honest and realistic evaluations, avoiding the traps of either self-criticism or self-delusion. Be honest about your challenges, and equally honest about your achievements. This means acknowledging the obstacles you face without dwelling on them, and celebrating even small victories without becoming complacent. The goal is to cultivate a balanced and realistic perspective on your journey.

Remember, celebrating successes and recognizing progress are not just separate activities; they are intertwined components of a holistic approach to achieving your goals. Celebrating successes reinforces positive behaviors and strengthens your self-efficacy, while recognizing progress keeps you motivated and focused on the journey, even during times of challenge or frustration. Together, they provide the fuel you need to continue moving forward, steadily and confidently, towards the fulfillment of your aspirations. By consciously incorporating these practices into your life, you will not only achieve your goals but also cultivate a deeper sense of self-awareness, self-compassion, and ultimately, self-acceptance, transforming the pursuit of your dreams into a journey of self-discovery and growth.

Building a Support System

Building a strong support system is paramount to achieving your goals and aspirations. The journey towards self-improvement and the attainment of ambitious targets is rarely a solitary endeavor. While self-belief and discipline are essential, surrounding yourself with the right people can significantly amplify your success and provide the necessary buffer against setbacks. A supportive network acts as a safety net, offering encouragement during difficult times, celebrating achievements, and providing valuable perspectives that you might miss on your own.

Think of your support system as a team of trusted advisors, cheerleaders, and mentors, each playing a crucial role in your journey. This isn't about seeking validation or approval, but about building a network of individuals who understand your aspirations, provide constructive feedback, and offer the emotional and practical support needed to overcome obstacles. The composition of this team will vary depending on your individual needs and the nature of your goals.

One crucial component is the presence of mentors. Mentors provide guidance based on their experience, offering valuable insights and strategies that you might not have considered. They act as seasoned navigators, charting a course through the often-uncharted waters of your ambitions. A mentor might be someone in your field who has already achieved success, a family member with a strong track record of resilience, or even a respected figure you admire from afar. The key is finding someone who understands your vision, provides constructive criticism, and can offer unwavering support.

The ideal mentor-mentee relationship is reciprocal. While the mentor provides guidance and shares their expertise, the mentee actively seeks feedback, implements suggestions, and shares their progress. This exchange strengthens the bond and creates a mutually beneficial relationship, fostering continued growth and understanding. Finding a mentor doesn't necessarily involve a formal arrangement. Sometimes, it's an organic connection forged through shared interests or mutual respect. Don't hesitate to reach out to individuals you admire and express your desire to learn from their experiences. The worst they can say is no, and even then, the experience of reaching out and articulating your ambitions will be a valuable learning opportunity in itself.

Beyond mentors, <u>trusted confidantes</u> play a vital role in providing emotional support and a sounding board for your ideas and concerns. These are the individuals who understand you deeply and offer unconditional support, regardless of the challenges you encounter.

They are the listeners, the shoulders to cry on, and the voices of reason during periods of self-doubt. These confidantes might be close friends, family members, or even a therapist who provides a safe and non-judgmental space for processing your emotions and experiences.

The importance of these relationships cannot be overstated. Sharing your struggles and celebrating your successes with trusted confidantes strengthens your resilience and reduces the feeling of isolation that can often accompany significant personal or professional challenges. Their support provides a counterbalance to self-doubt, allowing you to maintain perspective and persevere despite setbacks.

Remember, it is perfectly acceptable to seek help and support, particularly during challenging moments. It is a sign of strength, not weakness, to acknowledge the need for assistance and leverage the support of those around you.

Furthermore, building a support system also involves cultivating a network of <u>peers</u> who share similar goals and aspirations. These individuals offer not only encouragement but also a sense of community and shared experience. They understand the unique challenges and rewards inherent in pursuing your aspirations and can provide valuable perspectives and practical advice based on their own experiences. This might involve joining professional organizations, networking events, or online communities related to your field of interest.

Engaging with peers offers numerous benefits. It creates a sense of belonging and shared purpose, combating feelings of isolation and promoting a collaborative environment where you can learn from each other's successes and failures. The exchange of ideas, experiences, and support fosters a sense of camaraderie, motivating you to continue pushing forward. This shared journey can provide invaluable insights, resources, and inspiration, strengthening your resolve and enhancing your overall approach to achieving your objectives.

A powerful tool for building a supportive network is <u>active listening</u>. This involves not only hearing what others are saying but genuinely understanding their perspectives and experiences. It requires paying attention to both verbal and nonverbal cues, demonstrating empathy, and responding thoughtfully. Active listening fosters stronger relationships and encourages open communication, creating a space where individuals feel comfortable sharing their thoughts and concerns. When you demonstrate genuine interest in the lives and experiences of others, you build trust and strengthen your bonds, creating a more robust and supportive network.

Finally, remember that building a support system is an ongoing process. It requires nurturing and maintaining the relationships you have cultivated. This involves regular communication, active participation in shared activities, and a willingness to provide support in return. Cultivating these relationships takes time and effort, but the rewards are well worth the investment. By nurturing your support system, you create a lasting resource that will serve you well throughout your journey toward achieving your goals and aspirations. This proactive approach to building and nurturing relationships will create a resilient and responsive support system that can help you navigate unexpected challenges and celebrate your successes. Investing in these connections is an investment in your future.

Remember that building a strong support network is an iterative process. It's not a one-time event, but a continuous effort of nurturing existing relationships and forging new ones. Regularly evaluate your support system to see if it's still meeting your needs. Are there gaps you need to fill? Are there relationships that no longer serve you positively? Being honest with yourself about these things is crucial for maintaining a healthy and supportive network.

Furthermore, consider the diverse nature of support. Not all support is the same. Some people are great for brainstorming ideas, others provide emotional support, and still others offer practical help. Identify the different types of support you need and actively seek out people who can provide each. This could mean having one friend for brainstorming sessions, another for emotional venting, and a third for help with logistics or practical tasks. Diversifying your support system will ensure that you have the right resources available when you need them most.

Finally, don't underestimate the power of online communities. Numerous online forums, groups, and social media communities offer support and connection to people with similar interests and goals. These online spaces can provide a sense of community, offer valuable advice and insights, and help you feel less alone on your journey. However, remember to critically evaluate the information and support you receive online, as not all sources are equally reliable or trustworthy. Use your discernment and prioritize interactions with those who demonstrate genuine empathy and a commitment to positive support.

Remember that online communities should supplement, not replace, face-to-face interactions with trusted confidantes.

In conclusion, building a strong support system is not simply about surrounding yourself with people; it's about consciously cultivating relationships that offer diverse forms of support, understanding, and encouragement. It's a proactive and ongoing process that requires nurturing, evaluation, and a willingness to both give and receive help. By building a strong and multifaceted support system, you'll not only increase your chances of achieving your goals but also enrich your life with meaningful connections and unwavering support along the way. This network of supportive individuals will serve as a crucial cornerstone in your journey of self-discovery and achievement, providing the essential foundation for success. Remember, you don't have to face your challenges alone.

The strength of your support system can be the difference between achieving your goals and falling short. Invest in it wisely and watch your success flourish.

Chapter 5: Cultivating Lasting Personal Growth

Developing Self-Awareness

Developing self-awareness is the cornerstone of lasting personal growth. It's the ability to understand your thoughts, feelings, motivations, and behaviors, and how they impact your life and interactions with others. Without this crucial understanding, you're essentially navigating life blindfolded, reacting to circumstances rather than proactively shaping your destiny. This self-understanding isn't about self-criticism; it's about gaining a compassionate and objective perspective on yourself, allowing you to make conscious choices rather than being driven by unconscious patterns.

One of the most effective ways to cultivate self-awareness is through introspection. This involves taking time for quiet reflection, journaling, and mindful observation of your thoughts and feelings. Ask yourself probing questions: What triggers my emotional responses? What are my core values and beliefs? What are my strengths and weaknesses? What patterns consistently appear in my relationships and behaviors? Honest self-reflection, without judgment, allows you to identify areas for improvement and gain clarity on your motivations.

Journaling is an invaluable tool in this process. It provides a safe space to explore your thoughts and emotions without the pressure of immediate judgment. Write down your daily experiences, reflecting on your reactions and emotions. Analyze recurring themes or patterns. Over time, you'll begin to notice consistent trends in your behavior and emotional responses, providing valuable insights into your underlying beliefs and motivations. Try different journaling prompts, such as: "What was the most challenging situation I faced today, and how did I react?" or "What am I grateful for today, and why?"

Mindfulness practices are also crucial for developing self-awareness. Mindfulness involves paying attention to the present moment without judgment. Through practices like meditation or deep breathing exercises, you can cultivate a heightened awareness of your thoughts, feelings, and bodily sensations. This allows you to observe your internal world with greater clarity, identifying subtle shifts in your emotions and mental states before they escalate into overwhelming reactions. Even short periods of mindfulness meditation, just five to ten minutes daily, can significantly improve your capacity for self-observation.

Seeking feedback from trusted individuals is another powerful method for developing self-awareness. Choose people who know you well, are honest, and offer constructive criticism. Ask them for their honest perspectives on your strengths and weaknesses, your communication style, and your overall impact on others. Be open to hearing feedback, even if it's uncomfortable. Remember, the goal is self-improvement, and honest feedback, even if difficult to hear, is invaluable for growth. Frame this feedback as an opportunity to learn and grow, not as a personal attack.

Personality assessments, such as the Myers-Briggs Type Indicator (MBTI) or the Enneagram, can also provide valuable insights into your personality traits, preferences, and potential blind spots. These assessments offer a framework for understanding your natural tendencies and how they influence your actions and interactions. While these tools aren't definitive, they can be a useful starting point for exploring your personality and understanding your potential strengths and challenges. Remember that these assessments are meant to provide a general framework; they shouldn't define you.

Regular self-evaluation is key to maintaining and enhancing self-awareness. Set aside time regularly, perhaps weekly or monthly, to reflect on your progress. Analyze your accomplishments, challenges, and learning experiences.

Ask yourself: What worked well? What could I have done differently? What new insights have I gained? This ongoing process of self-reflection helps solidify your self-awareness and ensures you remain attentive to your growth and development.

Developing self-awareness is not a one-time achievement; it's a lifelong journey. The more you practice self-reflection, mindfulness, and seek constructive feedback, the more profound your understanding of yourself will become.

This ongoing process enhances emotional intelligence, improves decision-making, strengthens relationships, and ultimately empowers you to create a more fulfilling and meaningful life.

Embrace the journey of self-discovery; the rewards are immeasurable.

Understanding your emotional landscape is crucial for self-awareness. This involves identifying and understanding your emotional responses to various situations. Are you prone to anger, anxiety, or sadness? What triggers these emotions? By understanding your emotional triggers, you can develop strategies for managing them more effectively. This might involve practicing relaxation techniques, seeking professional help, or developing healthier coping mechanisms. The key is not to suppress your emotions but to understand their origins and develop healthier ways of expressing or processing them.

Another important aspect of self-awareness is understanding your values. Your values are your guiding principles, the things you believe are important and meaningful in life.

These values often influence your decision-making and behavior.

Take some time to identify your core values. What matters most to you? Is it family, creativity, learning, or something else? Once you've identified your values, ensure your actions and decisions align with them. This can provide a strong sense of purpose and direction in your life.

Self-awareness also extends to understanding your strengths and weaknesses. We all have unique talents and abilities, as well as areas where we need to improve. Identifying your strengths helps you leverage your potential. Recognizing your weaknesses enables you to address them effectively.

This involves honest self-assessment and a willingness to seek help or guidance when needed. Remember, acknowledging your weaknesses is not a sign of failure but an opportunity for growth and self-improvement. It's about striving for self-acceptance and improvement, not perfection.

Understanding your communication style is another critical element of self-awareness. How do you typically communicate with others? Are you direct or indirect? Assertive or passive? Understanding your communication style helps you to communicate more effectively and build stronger relationships. It allows you to tailor your communication approach to suit different situations and audiences. Consider seeking feedback from trusted sources on your communication style.

Are you a good listener? Do you communicate clearly and concisely? Do you express your needs and opinions effectively?

Recognizing your thought patterns is another vital aspect of self-awareness. What are the common themes or patterns in your thinking? Are you often negative or pessimistic? Do you engage in self-criticism or rumination? Understanding your thought patterns allows you to identify and challenge negative or unhelpful thinking habits. This might involve practicing cognitive restructuring or using positive affirmations to counter negative thoughts. This process takes time and practice, but the rewards are significant. By changing your thinking, you can change your behavior and emotional responses.

Finally, self-awareness involves understanding your physical needs. Are you getting enough sleep, exercise, and healthy nutrition? Ignoring your physical needs can have a significant impact on your mental and emotional well-being. Pay attention to your body's signals and make sure you're taking care of yourself physically. This might involve adjusting your diet, starting an exercise program, or prioritizing sleep. Remember, physical health and mental health are intricately intertwined.

The journey of self-awareness is a continuous process of exploration and discovery. There's always more to learn about yourself, and that's a beautiful thing. Embrace the process, celebrate your progress, and be patient with yourself. The more self-aware you become, the more empowered you'll be to create a life that is truly authentic and fulfilling. Remember, this isn't a race; it's a journey of continuous growth and understanding. Embrace the process and enjoy the rewards that come with increased self-knowledge.

Embracing Continuous Learning

Embracing continuous learning isn't merely about acquiring new skills; it's about cultivating a mindset that values growth and adaptation throughout life. It's a fundamental aspect of personal development, enabling us to navigate the ever-changing landscape of life with resilience and confidence. In a world of constant evolution, the ability to learn and adapt is no longer a luxury; it's a necessity. It's the key to unlocking our full potential and creating a future aligned with our aspirations.

Think of your brain as a muscle. Just as physical muscles atrophy without regular exercise, your cognitive abilities can stagnate if you don't actively challenge and expand them. Continuous learning keeps your mental muscles toned, sharp, and ready to tackle new challenges. It enhances your problem-solving skills, boosts creativity, and improves your overall cognitive function. The benefits extend far beyond the acquisition of new knowledge; they impact your overall well-being, contributing to increased self-esteem, reduced stress, and a greater sense of purpose.

One of the most effective ways to embrace continuous learning is to cultivate curiosity. Curiosity is the driving force behind exploration and discovery. It's the innate human desire to understand the world around us, to seek answers to our questions, and to push the boundaries of our knowledge. Ask yourself: What truly captivates my interest? What subjects have always intrigued me but I haven't had the opportunity to explore? By actively seeking out answers to your questions and engaging with subjects that pique your interest, you'll naturally cultivate a deeper understanding of yourself and the world.

Nurturing curiosity involves actively seeking out new experiences and challenges. Step outside of your comfort zone. Try a new hobby, learn a new language, or explore a subject you know little about. Attend workshops, seminars, or conferences related to your interests. Engage in conversations with people from diverse backgrounds and perspectives. The more you expose yourself to new ideas and perspectives, the more your curiosity will be ignited. Consider exploring subjects that initially seem daunting. The process of learning itself is often more rewarding than the final result.

The digital age provides unprecedented opportunities for continuous learning. Online courses, educational platforms, and vast online libraries offer access to a wealth of knowledge at your fingertips. Take advantage of these resources. Explore massive open online courses (MOOCs) offered by universities and educational institutions worldwide. Subscribe to podcasts or newsletters on topics that interest you. Engage with online communities and forums dedicated to learning and sharing knowledge. These online resources provide a flexible and convenient way to expand your knowledge and skills, fitting seamlessly into even the busiest schedules.

Reading is another invaluable tool for continuous learning. It's a powerful way to expand your horizons, learn new things, and cultivate a deeper understanding of the world. Make reading a regular part of your routine. Set aside time each day or week to read books, articles, or other materials related to your interests. Explore diverse genres and authors to broaden your perspectives. Don't limit yourself to fiction; dive into non-fiction books on topics that genuinely fascinate you. The breadth and depth of knowledge you can acquire through reading is limitless.

Remember that learning isn't confined to formal education or structured courses. You can learn from everyday experiences, from interactions with others, and from your mistakes. Pay close attention to your surroundings, actively seek out new experiences, and reflect on your daily encounters. Learn from your failures just as much as your successes.

Analyze situations where things didn't go as planned. What could you have done differently? What lessons can be learned from these setbacks?
Embrace these moments of learning as valuable opportunities for growth and self-improvement.

Continuous learning isn't a passive activity; it requires active engagement and participation. Ask questions, engage in discussions, and share your knowledge with others. Teaching others is a powerful way to consolidate your own understanding. The act of explaining a concept to someone else forces you to articulate your thoughts and identify any gaps in your knowledge. Find a study buddy or join a learning community to share your experiences and learn from others. The social aspect of learning can be immensely motivating and enriching.

Set realistic and achievable learning goals. Don't try to learn everything at once; focus on mastering one area or skill at a time. Break down larger goals into smaller, manageable steps. This will help prevent feeling overwhelmed and maintain your motivation. Celebrate your progress along the way. Acknowledge your accomplishments, no matter how small. Positive reinforcement helps keep your momentum going.

Regularly evaluate your learning journey. Reflect on what you've learned, what challenges you've faced, and how you've overcome them. This process of self-assessment helps identify areas for improvement and refine your learning strategies. Regular reflection also provides a sense of accomplishment and reinforces your commitment to continuous learning. By constantly evaluating your approach, you'll refine your methods and ensure you're consistently moving forward.

Continuous learning is a journey, not a destination. There will be times when you feel challenged, frustrated, or even discouraged. These moments are inevitable, and they are an integral part of the learning process. Don't let these setbacks derail your efforts. Embrace the challenges as opportunities for growth. Remember that setbacks are temporary, and the rewards of persistent learning are far greater than any temporary discomfort.

The benefits of continuous learning extend to every aspect of your life. It empowers you to adapt to change, overcome challenges, and create a more fulfilling and meaningful existence. It enhances your career prospects, strengthens your relationships, and improves your overall well-being. Embrace this lifelong journey of learning; it is a powerful investment in yourself and your future. The more you learn, the more you grow, the more you contribute, and the richer your life becomes. The possibilities are limitless, and the journey itself is incredibly rewarding. So, embark on this continuous learning journey with enthusiasm, and just watch yourself flourish my friend.

Practicing Self-Care and Well-being

Practicing self-care and well-being is not a luxury; it's a non-negotiable cornerstone of lasting personal growth. Just as a car needs regular maintenance to run smoothly, your mind and body require consistent nurturing to function optimally and support your journey of self-improvement. Neglecting your well-being undermines your efforts to grow, leaving you depleted and susceptible to burnout. Prioritizing self-care, however, fuels your progress, enhancing your resilience, focus, and overall capacity for growth.

One of the most fundamental aspects of self-care is physical well-being. This goes beyond simply avoiding illness; it's about actively cultivating a healthy lifestyle that supports your energy levels, mental clarity, and overall vitality. Begin with the basics: Prioritize regular physical activity. Find an activity you enjoy, whether it's brisk walking, swimming, cycling, dancing, or team sports. Aim for at least *30* minutes of moderate-intensity exercise most days of the week. The benefits extend far beyond physical fitness; regular exercise boosts mood, reduces stress, and improves sleep quality – all crucial for optimal cognitive function and emotional well-being.

Nutrition plays an equally critical role. Fuel your body with whole, unprocessed foods, focusing on fruits, vegetables, lean proteins, and whole grains. Limit your intake of processed foods, sugary drinks, and excessive caffeine. Hydration is also vital; aim to drink plenty of water throughout the day.

Nourishing your body with healthy foods provides the essential nutrients your brain and body need to function at their best, supporting both mental and physical energy levels.

Sleep is often underestimated but is a cornerstone of well-being. Aim for *7-9* hours of quality sleep each night. Establish a consistent sleep schedule, create a relaxing bedtime routine, and ensure your bedroom is dark, quiet, and cool. Adequate sleep allows your body and mind to repair and restore themselves, leaving you feeling refreshed, focused, and ready to tackle the day. Chronic sleep deprivation, on the other hand, impairs cognitive function, increases stress levels, and weakens your immune system, hindering your ability to grow and thrive.

Beyond the physical, emotional well-being is equally crucial. Learning to manage stress effectively is paramount. Chronic stress overwhelms the body and mind, leading to exhaustion, anxiety, and decreased cognitive function. Develop healthy coping mechanisms for stress, such as meditation, deep breathing exercises, yoga, spending time in nature, or engaging in hobbies you enjoy. Identify your personal stressors and develop strategies to mitigate them. This could involve setting boundaries, saying no to commitments that overwhelm you, or seeking support from friends, family, or a therapist.

Cultivating strong social connections is another vital component of emotional well-being. Humans are social creatures, and meaningful relationships provide a sense of belonging, support, and purpose. Nurture your relationships with loved ones, spend quality time with friends and family, and build new connections with people who share your interests. Social interaction reduces feelings of isolation and loneliness, boosting mood and overall well-being. Consider joining clubs, groups, or volunteering to expand your social circle and connect with like-minded individuals.

Mindfulness and self-compassion are crucial practices for emotional well-being. Mindfulness involves paying attention to the present moment without judgment. Practicing mindfulness, through meditation or simply observing your thoughts and feelings without getting carried away, enhances self-awareness and reduces stress and anxiety. Self-compassion involves treating yourself with kindness and understanding, especially during challenging times. Cultivating self-compassion helps you navigate setbacks with greater resilience and prevents self-criticism from undermining your progress.

Mental well-being extends to engaging in activities that bring you joy and a sense of purpose. Make time for hobbies, interests, and activities that nourish your soul and bring you a sense of fulfillment. These activities provide a break from the demands of daily life, reducing stress and promoting relaxation. Whether it's painting, reading, gardening, playing music, or spending time in nature, engaging in activities you enjoy boosts your mood, enhances creativity, and promotes a sense of accomplishment.

Spiritual well-being, for many, involves connecting with something larger than themselves. This could involve practicing religion, engaging in meditation, spending time in nature, or pursuing creative endeavors that tap into a sense of meaning and purpose. Connecting with something larger than yourself provides a sense of perspective, reduces feelings of isolation, and fosters a deeper sense of meaning and purpose in life. This connection can significantly enhance your overall sense of well-being and resilience.

Prioritizing self-care isn't selfish; it's essential for sustainable personal growth. By nurturing your physical, emotional, and spiritual well-being, you equip yourself with the resilience, energy, and focus necessary to pursue your goals and navigate life's challenges. Remember that self-care is not a one-size-fits-all approach. Experiment with different techniques and practices to discover what works best for you. Find what nourishes your mind, body, and soul, and make these practices a regular part of your routine. Consider keeping a journal to track your self-care practices and reflect on their impact.

Integrating self-care into your daily life might initially feel challenging. Start small. Begin by incorporating one or two self-care practices into your routine, gradually adding more as you build consistency. Schedule time for self-care, just as you would for any other important appointment. Treat it as a non-negotiable part of your day. Remember, you can't pour from an empty cup. By prioritizing self-care, you're investing in your well-being, strengthening your resilience, and ultimately fueling your journey towards lasting personal growth. The investment you make in yourself today will pay dividends in the form of increased energy, improved mental clarity, stronger relationships, and a greater capacity for achieving your goals.

Self-care isn't a quick fix; it's a continuous process of nurturing yourself physically, emotionally, and spiritually. It's about developing a mindful awareness of your needs and proactively addressing them. It's about listening to your body's signals, recognizing your emotional patterns, and consciously choosing actions that promote your overall well-being. Regular reflection is key to understanding your needs and adjusting your self-care practices accordingly. This involves consciously evaluating your routines and making necessary modifications to ensure that they continue to support your well-being. It might involve adjusting your exercise routine, modifying your diet, finding new ways to manage stress, or exploring new avenues for fostering meaningful connections.

Incorporating self-compassion into your self-care routine is also essential. Be kind to yourself; don't strive for perfection. There will be days when you slip up or neglect your self-care practices. This is perfectly normal. Instead of criticizing yourself, acknowledge your imperfections and gently guide yourself back on track. Remember that self-care is a lifelong journey, not a destination. There will be ups and downs, but the important thing is to remain committed to the process.

Regular self-reflection can enhance your self-care routine. Take time each week to reflect on your progress and make any necessary adjustments to your practices. Consider journaling or using a mindfulness app to facilitate this process. This reflective practice provides insights into your strengths and areas where you need further support.

It helps you to identify patterns and adjust your self-care strategy to best meet your evolving needs. Self-reflection encourages a continuous cycle of self-awareness, adjustment, and improvement, ensuring your self-care plan remains relevant and effective over time.

Finally, remember that seeking professional support is not a sign of weakness, but a sign of strength. If you are struggling with your mental or physical health, don't hesitate to reach out to a therapist, counselor, or doctor. They can provide guidance, support, and resources to help you navigate your challenges and cultivate lasting well-being. Professional help can provide you with tools and techniques to manage stress, improve your mental health, and address any underlying physical or emotional concerns that might be hindering your personal growth. Remember, prioritizing your well-being is an investment in your future, enabling you to pursue your goals with greater resilience, energy, and enthusiasm. The journey of personal growth is a marathon, not a sprint, and nurturing your well-being fuels your ability to run it effectively and sustainably.

Maintaining a Positive Mindset

Maintaining a positive mindset is not merely about thinking happy thoughts; it's a proactive and ongoing cultivation of a mental landscape that fosters resilience, optimism, and a sense of purpose. It's about consciously choosing to focus on the positive aspects of your life, even amidst challenges, and developing strategies to overcome negativity. This involves actively challenging negative thought patterns, practicing gratitude, and fostering self-compassion.

One of the most effective tools for cultivating a positive mindset is the conscious practice of gratitude. Taking time each day to reflect on the things you're grateful for, no matter how small, shifts your focus from what's lacking to what you already possess. This could be as simple as appreciating the warmth of the sun on your skin, the taste of a delicious meal, or the support of a loved one. Keeping a gratitude journal, where you write down three things you're grateful for each day, can significantly enhance this practice. The act of writing reinforces the positive emotions, solidifying the neural pathways associated with gratitude.

Furthermore, the practice of mindfulness plays a crucial role in maintaining a positive mindset. Mindfulness isn't about emptying your mind; it's about observing your thoughts and feelings without judgment. When negative thoughts arise, instead of getting swept away by them, acknowledge them, observe them, and gently let them pass. This non-reactive approach reduces the power of negative thoughts and allows you to maintain a more balanced perspective. Mindfulness meditation, even for a few minutes each day, can significantly enhance your ability to manage negative emotions and cultivate a more positive outlook.

Apps like Headspace or Calm provide guided meditations to support this practice.

Another vital aspect of cultivating a positive mindset is to actively challenge negative thought patterns. Negative thoughts often operate on autopilot, distorting reality and perpetuating feelings of anxiety, self-doubt, and unhappiness. When you notice a negative thought, challenge its validity. Ask yourself: Is this thought truly accurate? Is there another way of looking at this situation? What evidence supports this thought, and what evidence contradicts it? This process of cognitive restructuring helps you to replace negative thoughts with more balanced and realistic ones, reducing their impact on your emotions and overall well-being.

Self-compassion is also essential for maintaining a positive mindset. We are all imperfect, and life inevitably throws challenges our way. When facing setbacks, instead of criticizing yourself harshly, treat yourself with the same kindness and understanding you would offer a friend in a similar situation. Acknowledge your imperfections, accept your mistakes, and learn from them without self-recrimination. This compassionate approach allows you to navigate challenges with greater resilience and maintain a positive outlook, even when things don't go as planned.

Visualisation is another powerful tool for cultivating a positive mindset. This involves creating vivid mental images of your desired outcomes, imagining yourself achieving your goals, and feeling the positive emotions associated with success. Regular visualisation reinforces positive beliefs, boosts motivation, and increases your likelihood of achieving your goals. The act of vividly imagining yourself succeeding creates a mental blueprint that guides your actions and strengthens your commitment to your aspirations.

Positive affirmations are short, positive statements that you repeat to yourself regularly. These affirmations can help to reprogram your subconscious mind, replacing negative beliefs with positive ones. For example, if you struggle with self-doubt, you might repeat affirmations such as "I am capable," "I am worthy," or "I am confident."

Consistent repetition of these affirmations can gradually shift your mindset, fostering a greater sense of self-belief and confidence. It's important to choose affirmations that resonate with you personally and to say them with conviction.

Surrounding yourself with positive influences also significantly contributes to maintaining a positive mindset. This includes spending time with supportive friends and family who uplift and encourage you, engaging in activities that bring you joy and fulfillment, and limiting your exposure to negativity in the media or social interactions. Choose your social circles wisely; be selective about the people you spend time with. The energy of the people you surround yourself with has a significant impact on your mood and overall well-being.

Cultivating a positive mindset is not a passive endeavor; it's an active and ongoing process that requires consistent effort and self-awareness.

It's about consciously choosing to focus on the positive, challenging negative thoughts, and practicing self-compassion.

Regular reflection is key to identifying areas where you need to adjust your approach and to maintain a positive outlook throughout the ups and downs of life.

In addition to the practices mentioned above, fostering a sense of purpose plays a crucial role in maintaining a positive mindset. Having a sense of purpose provides a sense of meaning and direction in life, giving you something to strive for and a reason to overcome challenges. This could involve pursuing your passions, contributing to a cause you believe in, or setting meaningful goals that align with your values.

When you feel a sense of purpose, you're more likely to approach life's challenges with resilience and optimism.

Furthermore, practicing forgiveness, both of yourself and others, is essential for cultivating a positive mindset. Holding onto resentment and anger consumes energy and prevents you from moving forward. Forgiveness doesn't mean condoning harmful behavior; it means releasing the negative emotions associated with it, allowing you to heal and move on.

Forgiving yourself for past mistakes frees you from self-criticism and allows you to focus on the present. Forgiving others releases the burden of resentment and allows you to cultivate more positive relationships.

Another crucial aspect of maintaining a positive mindset is embracing imperfection. Life is messy, and things won't always go according to plan. Instead of striving for unrealistic perfection, accept that imperfections are part of the human experience. Embrace your mistakes as learning opportunities and strive for progress, not perfection. This approach reduces stress and increases resilience, enabling you to navigate challenges with a more positive and accepting attitude.

Learning to manage stress effectively is paramount to maintaining a positive mindset. Chronic stress depletes energy, increases negativity, and compromises mental well-being. Develop healthy coping mechanisms for stress, such as meditation, deep breathing exercises, spending time in nature, engaging in physical activity, or pursuing hobbies you enjoy. Regular exercise releases endorphins, which have mood-boosting effects. Spending time in nature has a calming effect, reducing stress hormones and promoting a sense of peace. Engaging in hobbies provides a welcome distraction from stressors, promoting relaxation and enjoyment.

Finally, remember that seeking professional support is not a sign of weakness but a sign of strength. If you're struggling to maintain a positive mindset despite your best efforts, don't hesitate to reach out to a therapist or counselor. They can provide guidance, support, and tools to help you address underlying issues that might be contributing to your negativity. They can teach you coping mechanisms, help you identify and challenge negative thought patterns, and develop strategies for building resilience and fostering a more positive outlook. Remember, cultivating a positive mindset is a journey, not a destination. It requires consistent effort, self-awareness, and a willingness to embrace the challenges along the way. By incorporating these practices into your life, you can create a mental landscape that fosters resilience, optimism, and a sense of purpose, empowering you to navigate life's challenges with greater ease and confidence.

Giving Back and Contributing to Others

The journey of personal growth isn't solely an inward-focused expedition; it's a deeply interconnected path that extends outwards, touching the lives of others and enriching the world around us. Cultivating lasting personal growth necessitates a reciprocal relationship between self-improvement and contribution to the greater good. Giving back isn't merely an act of altruism; it's a profound catalyst for our own continued development, fostering a sense of purpose, connection, and fulfillment that strengthens our inner selves.

One of the most rewarding aspects of giving back is the profound sense of purpose it instills. When we dedicate our time, energy, or resources to causes larger than ourselves, we transcend the limitations of our personal concerns and tap into a deeper wellspring of meaning. This sense of purpose isn't simply a feeling; it's a powerful motivator, providing direction and resilience in the face of challenges. Whether it's volunteering at a local soup kitchen, mentoring a young person, or donating to a charity aligned with our values, the act of contributing fosters a feeling of significance and belonging that strengthens our overall well-being.

The positive impact we have on others creates a ripple effect, positively impacting our own lives in ways we may not immediately recognize.

Beyond purpose, giving back cultivates genuine connection with others. When we engage in acts of service, we build bridges between ourselves and our communities. We form bonds with fellow volunteers, beneficiaries of our efforts, and the individuals and organizations we support. These connections create a sense of shared humanity, fostering empathy, understanding, and a deeper appreciation for the diverse experiences of others. This interconnectedness is a vital antidote to feelings of isolation and loneliness, promoting a sense of belonging and fostering stronger social support networks. These connections are not just transactional; they are relationships built on mutual respect, shared values, and a true and real common desire to make a difference.

Furthermore, contributing to others enhances our self-esteem and self-confidence. The experience of overcoming obstacles, mastering new skills, and making a positive impact on others instills a sense of accomplishment and self-efficacy. This boost in self-worth isn't just a temporary feeling; it's a fundamental shift in our perception of our capabilities. When we see ourselves as agents of positive change, we develop a stronger sense of self-belief, enhancing our resilience and motivation to continue pursuing personal growth. This is particularly true when we challenge ourselves to step outside our comfort zones and engage in activities that require new skills or push us beyond our perceived limitations.

The benefits of giving back extend beyond the immediate impact; they contribute to the creation of a more positive and resilient self. Acts of kindness and compassion stimulate the release of endorphins, natural mood boosters that reduce stress and enhance feelings of well-being. This physiological response is not only immediate but can have a lasting effect on our mental and emotional health. Regular acts of service can contribute to a more balanced and resilient emotional state, making us better equipped to handle life's inevitable ups and downs.

Giving back takes many forms, and finding the right avenue for contribution is a personal journey of discovery. It's crucial to identify areas that align with our passions, values, and skills. Some individuals find fulfillment in direct service, such as volunteering at homeless shelters, animal sanctuaries, or hospitals. Others might prefer to contribute through financial donations to causes they believe in, ensuring their resources are directed towards organizations that effectively address critical needs. Still others may find their purpose in using their professional skills to support non-profit organizations, offering pro bono services or mentorship.

Consider the diverse possibilities. Mentoring a young person can provide invaluable guidance and support, shaping the future while fostering a strong intergenerational connection. Participating in environmental cleanup initiatives contributes to the preservation of our planet and instills a sense of stewardship for the environment. Engaging in community-based projects can strengthen local bonds and build a stronger sense of community identity. The options are limitless, each offering a unique path to personal growth and societal contribution.

Finding your niche often involves experimentation. Try different approaches, exploring various volunteer opportunities, or supporting different organizations. This process of exploration isn't just about finding the perfect fit; it's about expanding our horizons, discovering new skills, and gaining a deeper understanding of our values and priorities. Don't be afraid to step outside your comfort zone; the most transformative experiences often lie beyond the familiar.

The impact of giving back transcends individual gains; it contributes to the creation of a more compassionate and just society. When we invest in our communities, we improve the lives of others and foster a more equitable and supportive environment for everyone. This collective effort creates a ripple effect of positive change, impacting not only those directly benefiting from our contributions but also shaping the overall societal fabric. The act of giving back is not just about individual growth; it's about contributing to the collective well-being.

However, it's vital to approach giving back with intentionality and sustainability. Avoid feeling pressured to overextend yourself or engage in activities that drain your energy or resources. Set realistic goals, prioritize activities that resonate with your passions, and pace yourself to ensure your efforts are sustainable in the long term.

Burnout can undermine the positive impacts of giving back, hindering both your personal well-being and the effectiveness of your contributions.

Remember that even small acts of kindness and generosity can have a profound impact. A simple gesture of helping a neighbor, offering words of encouragement to a colleague, or making a small donation to a worthy cause can have a significant positive effect. Don't underestimate the power of seemingly insignificant actions; these small contributions often accumulate, creating a powerful wave of positivity that transcends individual boundaries.

In conclusion, the cultivation of lasting personal growth is inextricably linked to the act of giving back and contributing to others. It's a reciprocal process that enriches both our inner selves and the world around us. By finding avenues for contribution that align with our values and passions, we tap into a deeper sense of purpose, connect with others, enhance our self-esteem, and contribute to the creation of a more compassionate and just society.

The journey of personal growth is not a solitary path but a shared endeavor, enriching the lives of those who give and receive.

Begin your new journey to embrace the transformative power of giving back, and watch as your own personal growth flourishes in tandem with the betterment of your community and the world.

Acknowledgments

This book wouldn't exist without the unwavering support and encouragement of numerous individuals. My deepest gratitude goes to those looking for change.

Glossary

Altruism: The principle or practice of unselfish concern for or devotion to the welfare of others.

Empathy: The ability to understand and share the feelings of another.

Self-Efficacy: One's belief in their own ability to succeed in specific situations or accomplish a task.

Resilience: The capacity to recover quickly from difficulties; toughness.

Well-being: The state of being comfortable, healthy, or happy.

Biography

Dr. *A*. Romani is an indie author and inspirational storyteller who's made waves in the literary world with his unique voice and compelling narratives. Armed with a doctorate that sharpened his research and communication skills, he's built a diverse portfolio spanning multiple genres—each infused with his signature blend of inspiration and insight. What sets Dr. Romani apart is his commitment to the transformative power of stories. He doesn't just put books out there; he creates movements of positivity and encouragement. Through his Indie Author works, he connects directly with readers seeking both entertainment and enlightenment. His books consistently resonate with audiences worldwide, offering comfort and motivation to those navigating their own life stories. Dr. Romani believes every story has the potential to change lives, and he's dedicated to being that beacon of hope— one book, one story at a time.

www.ingramcontent.com/pod-product-compliance
Lightning Source LLC
Chambersburg PA
CBHW071144300426
44113CB00009B/1072